MUSTACHE CUPS

Timeless Victorian Treasures

WITH PRICE GUIDE

Glenn Erardi &
Pauline C. Peck

Schiffer Publishing Ltd

4880 Lower Valley Road, Atglen, PA 19310 USA

DEDICATIONS

To my wife, Nancy.

To my three children: Kathy, my Victorian rose;
Captain Bill, my seafaring sailor;
and Sharon, my Irish nightingale.

Library of Congress Catalog Card Number: 99-63585

Type set in Galleria/Korinna BT
Designed by "Sue"

ISBN: 0-7643-0924-2
Printed in China
1 2 3 4

Published by Schiffer Publishing Ltd.
4880 Lower Valley Road
Atglen, PA 19310
Phone: (610) 593-1777; Fax: (610) 593-2002
E-mail: Schifferbk@aol.com
Please visit our web site catalog at
www.schifferbooks.com

This book may be purchased from the publisher.
Include $3.95 for shipping.
Please try your bookstore first.
We are interested in hearing from authors
with book ideas on related subjects.
You may write for a free catalog.

In Europe, Schiffer books are distributed by
Bushwood Books
6 Marksbury Rd.
Kew Gardens
Surrey TW9 4JF England
Phone: 44 (0)181 392-8585; Fax: 44 (0)181 392-9876
E-mail: Bushwd@aol.com

CONTENTS

ACKNOWLEDGMENTS

First and foremost, hats off to **Harvey Adams**, the intrepid Englishman who, around 1830, seized the dripping, drooping mustache by its handlebars and designed as well as manufactured the clever mustache cup. Without his derring-do, there'd be no book for you.

Without **Arthur and Nancy Young**, the book would be smaller, too. The Youngs graciously opened their home and mustache cup collection to us. About half of the entire mustache cups and accessories pictured are from their personal collection. And a special five stars to **Marion** whose gourmet cooking kept your authors very well fed and nourished while photographing part of the Youngs' collection.

Kathleen Tarr, owner of The Victorian Rose, was the consummate consultant throughout the long months of researching, writing, and valuing. She more than earned a baker's dozen of her favorite long-stemmed Victorian red roses.

Sharon Ross and **Julie Karcsinski** wore numerous helpful hats, from assisting in the care and cataloguing of the many mustache cups, to setting up and maintaining the computerware. Only they know how many times they responded to the rapacious ringing of the phone to hear the distaff side of your co-authors cry for help when her computer was being contrary.

Coast Guard Captain Bill Ross was too many states away to provide hands-on help. But he had a willing ear and offered oceans of practical, constructive criticism.

A Man and His Mustache

Three gold pencils to artist **Brenda Bechtel** whose mind's eye and creative fingers captured the essence of these Victorian treasures and accessories so beautifully throughout the book.

A sterling silver spoon (mustache, that is) to **Reed and Barton** for their help with researching the history of mustache spoons in the United States. Such spoons were advertised in their now famous 1885 catalogue, and again as recently as 1972.

Hands across the sea to **Harry Frost**, Curator of the Museum of Worcester Porcelain, who provided information, suggestions, and advice especially helpful to our research. Interestingly enough, he had never heard of mustache spoons or portable mustache guards. This supports our suspicions that these unique items were made only in the United States.

A prayer of thanks to **Eileen (Fay) Brooks,** Pauline's mother, who early on donated her own father's mustache cup as well as several other mustache cups and mugs to the collection. Her Irish eyes are surely smiling down on this book today.

A special thanks was earned the hard way by our editors, **Doug Congdon-Martin** and **Jennifer A. Lindbeck**. They evidenced patience and understanding as we juggled cups, commas, and captions in building this long-needed book. Without their expert advice and guidance we could have experienced great difficulty fleshing out the skeleton of an idea into the completed Victorian guide in hand.

And last but not least, heartfelt thanks to the following special people—**Betty Karcsinski** for loaning the photo of her father, a true Victorian gentleman, with his requisite mustache; **Geary Kaczorowski**, Cape Cod's best computer tutor, who saved the book when Pauline's computer crashed; **Lori Turner**, who kept house and hearth running efficiently while Pauline was lost in a world of words and a multiplicity of mustache cups; **Nancy Erardi**, Glenn's understanding wife, who never complained about his trips to Cape Cod to spend time photographing beautiful women—on Victorian mustache cups; and all the encouraging collectors, antique dealers, auctioneers, and librarians, too numerous to enumerate, who gave so willingly of their time, energy, and knowledge. You know who you are.

We owe you one!

PREFACE

My very first mustache cup was a birthday gift. That was a birthday two score and four years ago. When I learned that the cup was a true piece of Victoriana, I was delighted. The Victorian Age had long intrigued me. Its air of Pecksniffian propriety hid tantalizing secrets behind velvet draperies, bustling skirts, and handlebar mustaches. The mustache cup was a well-kept secret that had escaped my attention. And now I held one in my hand.

I soon learned that one was not enough. A few antique auctions, shows, and acquisitions later, I had a number of these Victorian treasures on display in my home. I was hooked. I was a collector. Little did I know then that many years later my family and friends would dub me "the Matriarch of Mustache Cups!"

My home at that time was a large old house on Penobscot Bay in Maine. The library was my personal security blanket—the room I retired to after The Images (my three children) were all hopefully asleep for the night. The room was walled with bookcases of old pumpkin pine that gleamed in the glow of the fireplace on frigid Maine nights.

One wall soon came to stand out from the rest. Books had been evicted to make room for the newest tenants, my mustache cups. My first mustache cup was hand painted with assorted fruits, mostly grapes. It enjoyed a prime location until it paled beside the elaborate gold decorations of some of my newer tenants. But it has held a special place in my heart for all these many years.

As my collection grew, so did visits from curious friends and neighbors. Most of them had never heard of a mustache cup, let alone seen one. I delighted in observing their reactions. Women marveled that men actually used some of the more delicate and ornate cups and saucers. Their questions flew: "Where did you find them? How did men use them without breaking them? How did they manage to hold the tiny handles? Who bought them—men or women?" Men inevitably gravitated to the "farmers' cups" that would hold at least a pint of tea or coffee. Men had questions too, especially men sporting mustaches of their own: "Are they still making them? Where can I find one? Why aren't men using them today?"

The question most frequently asked by both women and men is still often asked of me today: "Why do you collect men's mustache cups?" It was and is a good question. In my halcyon years I would just smile and reply coyly, "Because I can't well collect men to display on my shelves now, can I?" And that would suffice. Today my answer is more appropriate and, I hope, interesting as well.

With each new addition to my mustache cup collection, my fascination with these Victorian treasures grows. Some of my cups carry warm family memories. My mother unearthed my grandfather's silver mustache cup and saucer from an old family chest. The cup was etched with an "F" for Fay, the family name. My grandfather was Louis J. Fay, a well-known songwriter and publisher of ballads in Boston.

One of my prize pieces was given to me by a sister-in-law, back in my early days of collecting. It is a second black mark Irish Belleek (hand painted shamrocks and basket weave pattern) mustache cup and saucer that was part of a treasured family dinner set. The set had been hand-carried by her grandmother when she emigrated from Ireland aboard a steamship in the early 1900s.

Some years ago my youngest sister bought a thank-you gift for me in a charming antique shop. The owner assured her that it was an authentic mustache mug. When I eagerly unwrapped the package, I found a lovely mug. But it was a shaving mug, not a mustache mug. The antique dealer had made a mistake that many still make today. I cherish the mug and display it along with a few others I have acquired over the years. I often use it to show neophytes the difference between shaving mugs and mustache cups. It is pictured in the Introduction of this book.

My son and daughters, who learned at a very early age that mother's cups were "untouchables," have often gifted me with rare and precious finds during their travels. I have trained them well. I owe them so much for understanding my pride in my collection and for their many fine contributions. They truly are my "Images."

Over the years, my career in the publishing world has necessitated my living in a number of states. Transporting my mustache cup collection has been a major nightmare with each move. Although I personally wrapped or supervised the wrapping and unwrapping of each cup and saucer, I have lost a few to breakage. With my collection now in the hundreds, a few shouldn't matter, but they do.

My greatest loss was not due to moving. My collection had long outgrown the bookcase shelves. Also, to preserve their beauty and condition, the cups had to be displayed under glass. So, I commissioned a young cabinetmaker to design a Victorian-style cabinet. His design was superb. He created a warm cherry cabinet with lighted glass shelves, sides, and doors. But my addiction to collecting these Victorian treasures would not be satiated and soon that cabinet was as tightly packed as a Victorian corset!

My cabinetmaker designed a companion piece. The first cabinet was seven feet tall. This cabinet was half the height and seven feet long. In addition, it had a glass top for interesting viewing. Soon the second cabinet was well on the way to being filled. Then one night I was awakened from a deep sleep to a roaring sound that seemed to go on and on and on. Yes, it was the newer mustache cup cabinet. One of the long glass shelves had buckled under the weight of too many cups. It broke in the middle, sending cups and saucers sliding down and out. The "out" was what saved me from a really devastating loss. I had forgotten to latch the two glass doors, and they had swung open, allowing the cups to slide down and out onto the cushioning carpet.

After an appropriate "mourning" period, I had the glass shelves replaced with much sturdier glass, counted my losses, and resumed collecting. I have yet to replace one cup I personally treasured. I had found it in Scotland. It was left-handed and was hand painted with a magnificent red stag with full antlers. I haven't given up hope for I still "have miles to go before I sleep."

Over these many years of collecting mustache cups, I have learned what I could the hard way. The only book devoted to mustache cups was Dorothy Hammond's book published in 1972 and now out of print. The book was most helpful in many ways, but could not really help me with dating and valuing the pieces in my collection. My Images, tired of my constant complaining of the amount of research I had to do for each new acquisition, finally responded in exasperation, "You're a writer. Write a mustache cup book yourself!" But I never seemed to find the time.

Then fate, in the form of my co-author, came courting. Everything was right. I had the time, the interest, and the knowledge. And I certainly had the cups! Glenn had the knowledge, experience, and contacts in addition to being an excellent photographer. So we solemnly said our "I do's" and entered into the holy bond of co-authorship.

I enlisted the use of the mustache cup collection of my dear friends, Arthur and Nancy Young, in addition to my own. The Youngs' collection is more extensive than mine and their generosity in allowing us to photograph and catalogue many of their cups and related memorabilia is greatly appreciated by Glenn and me. While we were planning the book, Glenn was at least nipped by the mustache cup bug and acquired a few cups and accessories himself. He claims he's not hooked, but he sure has the virus!

I sincerely hope that this long overdue book will be of help to collectors, antique dealers, librarians, and all who have an interest in porcelain, pottery, silver, and Victoriana. Mustache cups are truly cross-collectibles. A representation belongs in every ceramics or silver collection.

I look forward to continuing my research on mustache cups and related memorabilia to include cups and items not covered in this book. We have many more mustache cups to photograph and evaluate as well as more associated items. I would also welcome hearing from collectors who would be interested in contributing photographs of cups (with pertinent data) from their personal collections for possible inclusion in a second book. Please include a stamped, self-addressed envelope if a reply is in order.

Pauline C. Peck
P. O. Box # 1851
Mashpee, MA 02649

Victorian Dandy
Courtesy of Karcsinski family

Mustaches and Music

Two Victorian Swingers

Proper Victorian

INTRODUCTION

History of the Mustache

Who "invented" the mustache? To date, no stalwart soul has claimed the credit. But mustaches, with or without beards, have been around since the beginning of time. Their shape, size, and even condition have waxed and waned with the times, from the bushy handlebar associated with the boisterous prospectors of the Gold Rush to the diminutive hirsute patch on the upper lip as sported by comedian Charlie Chaplin.

For our purposes, let's begin with the 1600s when perukes (wigs) were in fashion and facial hair was losing its roots. By the time the 1700s rolled around, most men were clean-shaven. History reveals that the signers of the Declaration of Independence all eschewed facial hair, and no United States President preceding Abraham Lincoln had sported a mustache, beard, or both. President Lincoln only grew his beard between his nomination and inauguration—at the suggestion of a young girl who thought it might improve his appearance. All the succeeding Presidents, from Ulysses S. Grant to Howard Taft (with the exception of William McKinley), were mustachioed men, four of them having accompanying beards. Since President Taft, however, all United States Presidents have been clean-shaven. One might speculate if clean-shaven men are apt to be perceived as more honest and trustworthy than are men with mustaches.

Villains have been known to twirl the ends of their long, curled mustaches when pleased with anticipated prospects, a la silent filmdom's episodes of "Perils of Pauline!" Lotharios have been depicted as sporting neatly trimmed mustaches as they wooed and won fair maidens. Santa Claus, the jolly old elf with the flowing white mustache and beard, still wins the hearts of children of all ages. His reputation is certainly as pure as the proverbial snow. And Rhett Butler, as depicted so well by Clark Gable, combined the best and the basest of human nature. Yet, who could picture him without his crowning glory?

"Oh, your father's mustache!" was a popular childhood taunt of the 1800s. What spurred the growth in popularity for mustaches in the Victorian years? A number of possibilities have been proffered.

In England, men began to sport a Napoleon shortly after the Franco-Prussian War. In the United States, the popularity of the mustache among men in all ranks of the armed services, as well as civilian males, appears to have followed close on the heels of the War with Mexico (1846-1847) and the ensuing Gold Rush era. Prospectors found it difficult to keep clean-shaven during their arduous journeys through wilderness areas and working in mines. So mustaches and beards grew long and unkempt for months and even years. Along with these events, we can't omit the universal assumption that hairiness in men often indicates the extent of their virility. Whether a valid assumption or not, mustaches and manliness walked hand in Victorian hand.

Whatever the cause or causes, most gentlemen in Europe and the United States in the 1800s sprouted and cultivated mustaches and/or beards. They remained in vogue until about 1890 when the beards began to disappear. But the more popular mustaches lingered on. Around the time of World War I, even the mustaches began to lose favor. Today, most men adopt them or not to suit their individual needs and personalities.

Back in the 1800s and early 1900s, however, the widespread popularity of mustaches presented the male population with a rash of problems. Solving these problems gave rise to a whole new marketing area. Gentlemen' s mustaches required protection, care, and cultivation or they would grow as wild and woolly as those worn by bewhiskered prospectors and cowboys. So mustaches needed to be washed, combed, curled, waxed, and even dyed. "Old Reliable Hair and Whisker Dye" surged in sales along with mustache combs, brushes, curling irons, spirit heaters, oils, wax, and hairnets. The nets held the waxed and curled mustaches securely in place while the gentlemen slept. Vanity, thy name was Victorian man!

Another major problem soon cropped up. When dapper gentlemen sipped tea, coffee, or soup, mustaches often became soiled and stained. Also, the hot beverages tended to melt the waxed mustaches with seriocomic results. Picture the melted wax dripping down chins into cups while handlebars sagged and drooped into cups and soups! As Holly Golightly would say, "Quelle mess!"

History of the Mustache Cup

Around 1830, news of an invention from the fertile mind of a young potter reached the drawing room circuit around England. The dandies were delighted! The gentlemen were jolly well pleased. The invention was the mustache cup. Who was the inventor? Harvey Adams of Longton, Stoke-on-Trent, where he designed and manufactured the first known mustache cup. Word of the new invention spread and eventually every well-known potter was producing mustache cups.

In 1860, a Mr. Hammersley became Adams' partner until 1875 when the inventor retired. The Hammersley family continued to manufacture all kinds of china under the name of Hammersley & Company at Longton. Today, Hammersley & Co. is part of Royal Worcester, Ltd., Royal Porcelain Works. In correspondence with the curator of the Museum of Worcester Porcelain, we were surprised to learn that they have only three mustache cups and saucers in their collection, two from the 1880s and one from the 1890s. Incidentally, the curator spells mustache as moustache. You will find both versions acceptable, but the preferred spelling is without the "o."

The very early mustache cups were often referred to as "Napoleons and Saucers," due to the nickname used for the mustaches and beards worn by Englishmen at that time. We are not sure when this nickname disappeared, but it was almost lost to history.

What exactly **is** a mustache cup? Basically, it is a Victorian cup (and saucer) that was designed especially for mustachioed men. What sets it apart from a regular cup? Each mustache cup has a ledge, called a mustache guard, that has one semi-circular opening against the side of the cup. As a gentleman sipped his hot tea or coffee through the opening, his mustache rested safely on the guard. The guard protected the mustache from becoming stained or soiled. It also kept the wax on some mustaches from melting into the hot beverage. Many mustache guards are shaped like a mustache; some are very ornately designed; some are curled up for additional protection. Most guards are applied to the cup in much the same way as handles are applied. A rare few are molded as part of the cup mold. An even rarer few are molded and raised. But all have one thing in common. Each guard has only **one** semi-circular opening.

We can hear the supportive "Amen!" from collectors at this point. Long a bane with collectors is the rampant confusion of **shaving mugs** with mustache cups. Too many people, including many antique dealers, are not sure of the differences. Certain types of shaving mugs have a ledge of sorts that has **three** or more small round holes. Soapy water drained through these round holes as a gentleman used a shaving brush and razor to remove his whiskered growth. Study the photos on pages 13 and 14 and read the captions. These are different views of a few types of shaving mugs. We guarantee that a gentleman trying to use these cups to sip hot beverages would suffer some debilitating damage to his pride and paunch!

In the early years of their production, most mustache cups were personalized. They were usually given as gifts to male family members from female members. We suspect that is why so many are ornate, delicate, and pleasing to the eye rather than strictly utilitarian. Many mustache cups carried inscriptions that included monograms, names, messages, rhymes, old sayings, and even prayers. In Queen Victoria's day it was considered in good taste to give a favorite male a mustache cup inscribed: "To Papa," "Forget me not," "Love the Giver," "I Love You Best," "A Present," "May Your Fortunes Blossom," or "To Brother," to name only a few of the most popular inscriptions. Eventually sets—a mustache cup for the man and a matching cup for the woman (without a guard, of course)—were made. These are referred to as His and Hers sets. Some were inscribed "Husband" and "Wife." These inscribed sets are scarce and considered rare. Wedding sets to give a bride and groom soon evolved. Interestingly enough, the two sets we have were well used as noted by the wear to the gold.

Designs, other than inscriptions on mustache cups, covered a wide range of interests. Many mustache cup collectors prize ornate cups with lavish gold designs. Gilding was widely used, even on cups with a fairly simple style. The interiors of many cups gleam with gold as do the mustache guards and handles. Heavy gold floral clusters are not at all unusual. Very few cups are found without some gold representation. Victorians did know how to "gild the lily."

Although the majority of mustache cups are hand painted, portraits and figural decals are frequently found as are seasonal scenes showing flora and fauna. A few scarce cups depicting dogs, horses, and deer have turned up at auctions recently, bringing higher prices than was anticipated. A number of mustache cups feature hand-painted exotic flowers and birds; some cups are decorated with geometric designs in strikingly bold colors. Cups with decalcomania and transfer designs are not uncommon, but are frequently combined with hand painted designs and borders.

Roses, a Victorian favorite, appear on many cups. The hand-painted roses far outshine those found on decals or transfers. The roses range in color from deep reds to pale white with soft pink hues. A few cups with hand painted yellow roses have been found. These are striking. Cups decorated with cobalt are as popular today as they were in the 1800s. A few outstanding cups with an overall gold and cobalt design are prized items in some collections. Spongeware and spatter designs were favorites with Victorians almost as much as lustre. Lustre cups reached the peak of their popularity in the 1880s. Some very unusual lustre colors can be found scattered throughout the cups pictured in this book. And many cups feature delicate designs using pale lavender, yellow, or pink. There is something to suit everybody's taste in the designs of mustache cups from the bold and striking to the delicate and subdued.

As seasoned collectors know, commemorative and souvenir mustache cups can be acquired at auctions, shops, or shows. Many of these appear to have been made to order in Germany for the United States market, especially the souvenir cups. Quite a number of the cups are mementos of places or buildings not widely known throughout the states. Cups bearing insignias of fraternal organizations were made but are very scarce. None are pictured here.

Many mustache cups are not marked. But marks found on ceramic cups were impressed, incised, underglaze, or overglaze. European potters usually marked their cups. But ceramic cups made in the United States were rarely marked until the 1900s. American wares bearing a potter's mark are very scarce and considered highly collectible. English wares showing the mark "England" were usually made after 1891; however, some English potters used the word England long before that year.

Why is 1891 so important? That was the year that the McKinley Tariff Act took effect. This Act required all articles imported to the United States to be marked with the name of the country of origin. Up until that time many mustache cups were totally unmarked, bearing neither the mark of the manufacturer nor the country. You will note that many Oriental cups and saucers in this book are listed as "country unknown." There are several reasons for this. Many Oriental mustache cups were made in cottage factories or by various family units. Some of these are unmarked and some are marked with Oriental characters that we could not interpret. Nippon pieces are well marked, but one must study the Nippon marks carefully, as too many of them have been reproduced and are fake marks.

Marks of many European potters changed frequently over the years from about 1700 on, but the dates of change are well documented and are easy to identify. Before 1842, most of the English wares were marked only with the trade name of a particular pattern. From 1842 through 1883, a system of marking articles (ceramics, wood, metal, etc.) was required by the British Patent Office. The diamond-shape Registry Mark included the year, month, and day on which the article was made as well as the type of ware. This registration marking has been a boon to both dealers and collectors.

Mustache cups are found in all sizes from miniature to the very large farmers' cups. The large cups hold a pint or more of tea or coffee. Miniatures are very scarce and are considered a rarity. Mustache cups can also be found in a variety of shapes. Unusual shapes such as seashell, kettle, heart, square, octagonal, hexagonal, brandy snifter, and thunderjug command higher prices than the more common shapes. A few of the mustache cups have pedestals or are footed, especially the kettle shape. Most kettles are four-footed, but the rare three-footed can be found if you persevere. One is pictured in this book.

Mustache cup handles are quite varied and fascinating. Throughout the book you will find examples of cherub (rare), half-scissors, question mark, rope, bamboo, fan, shell, and so on. Captions with the photos will help you to identify most of the unusual handles.

All mustache cups with the exception of large mugs, steins, and possibly a few large kettle-shape, originally had matching saucers. The earliest cups had very deep saucers. Later, saucers became more compatible with those used today. In the latter part of the Victorian era, many fine dinner sets included at least one mustache cup and saucer and one demitasse cup and saucer. Tea sets, breakfast, and luncheon sets often included a mustache cup. But mustache cups do not seem to have been part of chocolate sets. We find that unusual since hot chocolate was a favorite Victorian beverage. Perhaps it was more popular with the distaff side than with the Victorian gentlemen.

Left-handed mustache cups were produced by some of the potters, but the true Victorian left-handed cups are extremely rare as they are scarcer than the proverbial hens' teeth! Reproductions were manufactured from about the 1940s on. Most of these valid reproductions are marked and were not meant to deceive; therefore they are not considered fakes. Fakes have been reproduced with all attempts to conceal their true origins. Some are marked with fake R.S. Prussia or R.S. Germany marks as well as fake Nippon marks, among others. And some fakes are labeled JB 1200 or Brandenburg with an anchor. (See Chapter Six for examples of valid reproductions versus total fakes.) Don't be too chagrined to find a fake or two in your own shop or collection. We found them in ours. Most were gifts from unsuspecting friends and family, but we do admit to being misled in a few of our own early purchases. So, caveat emptor! Honesty may be good for the soul, but it sure can hurt the seller's piggy bank.

Serious collectors are probably well aware that mustache glasses, beakers, spoons, and portable mustache guards were also manufactured and used. We have not been fortunate enough to even see a glass or beaker, but we do have spoons and guards as well as other accessories. You can learn more about these in Chapter Seven. The only sterling silver left-handed mustache spoon that we have ever had is pictured in that chapter. It is the perfect gift for that special, left-handed, mustachioed man who has everything!

Mustache cups and saucers have been quietly collected for years. Forty or more years ago it was relatively easy to acquire a beautiful and rare example for a reasonable price. That is not quite true today. As highly prized cups have been fading from the marketplace, the prices have gradually increased. In just the last few years, prices have escalated more rapidly. We suspect that some of the most desirable cups have been squirreled away by a bushel or so of avid collectors. Just this past year we heard tell of a man who boasts of having over 10,000 in his private collection. And we just happen to have a mustache shaped bridge he might be interested in buying!

A Consummate Collection of Mustache Cups

Since Victoriana has come into its own in recent years, Victorian items are highly desirable. Consequently, mustache cups are coming out of the cupboards and collections to be put on the auction block. When one first catches the mustache cup fever, almost any mustache cup, with or without saucer, in reasonably good condition is highly collectible. The longer one collects, the more discriminating he/she becomes. If possible, try to find cups representative of the different categories. Look especially for molded mustache guards, cherub handles, footed kettles, demitasse cups, sets, lustres, portraits, presentation cups with unusual inscriptions, miniatures, and left-handed cups.

No collection is considered really good without cups from various potters. You will want to acquire cups from different countries, including France, Germany, England, Ireland, Japan, and the United States. Study the marks in Chapter Six. Look for these potters' marks as you acquire your mustache cups. A good collection should have cups made of porcelain, earthenware, and silver or other metals. Any sets you might come across will be a welcome addition. Various sizes and shapes should also be included. Miniatures will prove to be the hardest to come by and true left-handed cups will be next to impossible.

The really serious collector will strive to number at least one Irish Belleek, R.S. Prussia, Majolica, Royal Worcester, Nippon, Dresden, Meissen, Sunderland Lustre, Royal Crown Derby, and Rose Medallion among his/her more obtainable mustache cups. This may sound impossible, given all you have just read. But you can do the impossible if you try. We did!

How to Collect Mustache Cups

Collecting mustache cups requires dedication as they are virtually a Victorian secret—unfamiliar to many people, even those who may have inherited one. Ask a friend or neighbor to tell you what a mustache cup is. Nine out of ten facial expressions will be as blank as a teacher's chalkboard during vacation time. If you aren't dedicated, then you'll never find the time, diligence, perseverance, knowledge, shoe leather, and nose to ferret them out, let alone the cold hard cash to claim them. If we haven't discouraged you, leaving more for us devotees to find, then we offer the following tips.

Begin by learning all you can about mustache cups and their marks to arm you against the fakery. If the price seems rather low for a true treasure, then it is probably a fake. Our rule of thumb is, when in doubt, don't buy. You might miss a real bargain, but you might also pay a high price for a forgery. Start your search at established antique shops that have a good reputation to maintain. Group shops are a good starting point due to the variety of their wares. If you come across a mislabeled shaving mug, alert the dealer. The dealer may not thank you, but collectors everywhere will.

When you do find a cup, check it carefully. Look for chips, cracks, flakes, repairs, hairlines, and heavy wear. Check the mark/backstamp if there is one. Is it familiar? If not, can you find it in this book or a book of marks? If there is a saucer, look it over carefully to see if it is a true match. The cup should fit snugly in the saucer, not slide around. Then do a finger test. Hold the cup firmly in your hands, close your eyes, and feel the rim, decoration, and handle with your fingertips. Sometimes the fingers can see flakes or chips better than the eyes. When you are satisfied with the item, talk with the dealer. Is his/her price firm? Can you bargain? Be sure you have a maximum price fixed firmly in your mind and stick to it. No item is worth filing for bankruptcy!

Auctions are often an exciting way to pick up mustache cups. You might find them listed in with the smalls or the collectibles. However, don't count on it. Often times they are not listed at all. Most importantly, **preview the auction**. Never, ever bid on a mustache cup or any other item that you have not had the chance to touch and examine. Items can look great when displayed by the auctioneer or assistant. Imperfections and fakes cannot be positively discerned at a distance. Most auctioneers do warn you if an item has some damage, but all items are auctioned **as is**. Also, listen to the auctioneer's words attentively. An item described as in the "Dresden style" is usually not true Dresden.

Sometimes you can do very well with prices at an auction. The buying audience is made up of dealers, collectors, and occasional buyers. Try to identify the dealers. They are usually known to the auctioneer and make frequent purchases. Their highest bid will always be lower than a collector's will. They have to resell the item at a profit. Collectors do not. And do go to auctions armed with your own type of wrapping and a box for your purchases. Any breakage after you buy is on you, not the house!

Try antique shows. Prices will not be low unless the dealer has had a slow day, but you can find treasures at some shows. Just follow all the caveats you would use for purchases at an antique shop. Antique shows do usually offer a great variety of items, and dealers often display items that are harder to sell within the limited confines of their shop.

Now and then you can find a hidden treasure at a yard or estate sale. But you must go early. And in most cases a dealer will have been there before you. Dealers go to yard sales before the birds are even awake. One man we know picked up a diamond Tiffany pin at a yard sale for fifty cents. He was an early bird dealer. Enough said?

The internet is the most innovative and newest source for acquiring mustache cups. Although antique shop

SM: Germany, c. 1892-1912, decals, Mark 119.

SM interior: drain holes in brush ledge, preceding SM.

SM and pin tray: Austria, c. 1892+, decals, marked, "Austria."

Chapter One

CERAMIC MUSTACHE CUPS

Welcome to the visual world of mustache cups and saucers in all their colorful Victorian glory. Chapter One presents those ceramic mustache cups that survived the passage of time with matching saucers intact. A very few pictured cups have saucers that appear to be mismatched. These are identified in the captions.

Mustache cups with matching saucers are those most highly prized by collectors. If they are considered to be rarities and are in perfect condition, their intrinsic and monetary value soars. But a word of caution is necessary. Total fakes and reproductions do exist, unfortunately. A very few of them have been included in this and the second chapter to afford comparison with true Victorian era pieces and to keep you on your toes! See if you can detect them before reading the captions.

You will find that a picture is not always worth a thousand words. It does not always offer immediate identification. But then, neither does the object in hand. Some of these contemporary cups and saucers require much experience and research to afford proper recognition. The accompanying captions reflect this problem.

Many of the captions that read "country unknown" are not at all a mystery to this collector. An educated guess could be readily supplied. But unmarked cups and saucers are best labeled "unknown" for the purists, and to keep the records straight.

Advanced collectors of these Victorian treasures do not consider their collection complete without cups marked Belleek, Imari, Majolica, R.S. Prussia, Royal Bayreuth, Minton, Wedgwood, etc. And a left-handed cup bearing one of these marks is a collector's dream. But the dream can never take wing if the cup is seriously flawed or poorly repaired. It remains a caterpillar on the leaf of reality.

MC/S: France, c. 1891-1900, HP unusual colors, applied MG, Mark 1, $275-300.

MG: scalloped, with gold dsn, preceding MC.

MC/S: country unkn, c. 1855-1865, HP w/silver and gold, applied MG, unmarked, $200-225.

MC/S: country unkn, c. 1860-1870, HP and transfer, applied MG, unmarked, $125-135.

MC/S: Germany, c. 1902 +, HP and decals, applied MG, Mark 116, $110-125.

MC/S: country unkn, c.1850-1860, HP to mold, applied MG, unmarked, $175-200.

MC/S: country unkn, c. unkn, HP rare geometric dsn, applied recessed MG, unmarked, $250-300.

MG: rare geometric dsn, preceding MC.

MC/S: USA, c. 1904+, HP, applied MG, Lefton China, $60-65.

MC/S: Germany, c. 1880-1890, HP wedding band dsn, applied MG, Mark 5, $110-130.

MC/S: Japan, c. 1891-1921, HP, Art Nouveau dsn, applied MG, Mark 47, $275-300.

MC/S: country unkn, c. 1870-1880, HP applied gold dsn, applied MG, unmarked, $175-200.

MC/S: Germany, c. 1903-1913, HP, applied MG, Mark 6, $175-200.

MC/S: Germany, c. 1892-1900, HP, applied dsn, deep saucer, applied MG, marked, "Germany" in tiny circle, underglaze, $175-195.

MC/S: country unkn, c. 1880-1890, HP, applied dsn, applied MG, unmarked, $150-160.

Demitasse MC/S: country unkn, c. 1875-1880, HP, applied MG, unmarked, $200-250.

Rare miniature MC/S: country unkn, c. 1900+, HP, question mark handle, applied MG, Mark 7, $400-450.

MC/S: USA, c. 1949+, decals, twisted handle, applied MG, Mark 8, $65-70.

Rare square MC/S: country unkn, c. 1880-1883, HP, applied MG in corner of cup, unmarked, $225-275.

MC/S: Germany, c. 1903-1913, decals, applied MG, Mark 6, $180-200.

MM/S: Germany, c. 1890, HP, applied MG, Mark 9, $150-170.

Rare square MC/S: country unkn, c. 1875-1885, HP, pearlescent lustre, ornate handle, four-footed, applied MG, unmarked, $225-250.

MC/S: Germany, c. 1902, HP and decals, applied MG, Mark 10, $150-175.

MC/S: Japan, c. 1890-1921, HP, applied MG, Mark 11, $225-250.

MG: HP dsn, preceding MC.

MC/S: country unkn, c. 1875-1885, HP, applied MG, unmarked, $140-150.

MC/S: Germany, c. 1892-1910, HP and decals, applied MG, marked, "Three Crown China, Germany," $150-175.

MC/S: country unkn, c. 1885+, HP and decals, rare salmon color, wishbone handle, applied MG, Mark 12, $150-175.

MC/S: country unkn, c. 1885-1890, HP, applied MG, unmarked, $110-120.

MC/S: Germany, c. 1891-1900, HP, rare pearl yellow and deep purple lustre, applied decoration, applied MG, marked, "Germany" in red, $145-165.

Rare heart MC/S: Germany, c. pre World War I, HP and transfer, wishbone handle, applied MG, rare Mark 13, $1,100-1,300.

MG: heart-shaped, preceding MC.

MC/S: France, c. 1870-1880, HP, unusual thunderjug shape, rectangular handle, applied MG with deep apron, unmarked, $175-200.

Demitasse MC/S: country unkn, c. 1875-1885, HP, unusual dsn, rare molded and raised MG, unmarked, $300-325.

MC/S: France, c. 1891-1904, HP and transfer, applied MG, Mark 14, $275-325.

MC/S: France, c. 1876-1889, HP wedding band dsn, applied MG, Mark 16, $300-325.

MC/S: England, c. 1889, pink pattern dsn, half-scissors handle, applied MG, Mark 15, $275-325.

MG: pink pattern dsn, preceding MC.

MC/S: Germany, c. 1901-1910, HP and decals, applied MG, Mark 5l, $150-175.

MC/S: Germany, c. 1887+, HP and transfer, ornate handle, applied MG, Mark 22, $175-200.

Square MC/S: country unkn, c. 1880-1890, HP, unusual use of color, applied MG, unmarked, $300-325.

MG: deep in corner of preceding MC.

MC/S: France, c. 1896-1905, HP gold matte finish, applied MG, Marks 17-18, $350-375.

MG: HP gold dsn, preceding MC.

MC/S: France, c. 1906, HP matte finish, applied MG, Marks 19-20, $350-375.

Hexagon MC/S: Germany, c. 1900, HP unusual dsn, hexagon pedestal, applied MG, Mark 52, $175-200.

MM/S: country unkn, c. 1870-1875, HP exotic dsn, applied MG, unmarked, $200-225.

MG: HP and raised, preceding MC.

MC/S: England or USA, c. 1863+ (England); 1876+ (USA), HP, applied MG, Mark 21, $250-275.

Farmer's MC/S: England, c. 1968+, transfer dsn, applied MG, marked, "Ironstone, Staffordshire, England," $75-100.

MC/S: Oriental, country unkn, c. unkn, HP (possibly over stencil), applied MG, marked with red Oriental characters, $300-325.

MG: HP dsn, preceding MC.

MC/S: Germany, c. 1887+, HP and decal, applied MG, Mark 22, $125-135.

MC/S: country unkn, c. 1870-1880, HP, applied MG, unmarked, $150-165.

Farmer's MC/S: England, c. 1930+, transfer, applied MG, Marks 23-24, $200-225.

MG: large and flat, preceding MC.

MC/S: country unkn, c. 1865-1875, HP and decals, applied MG, unmarked, $160-180.

Demitasse MC/S: Germany, c. 1887-1902, HP unusual colors, applied MG, Mark 25, $225-250.

MC/S: Germany, c. 1891-1900, HP, unusual weave dsn, applied MG, Mark 33, $175-200.

MC/S: Germany, c. 1901-1910, HP and decals, modified pedestal, applied MG, Mark 26, $200-225.

MC/S: country unkn, c. 1875-1885, HP and sgn, applied MG, unmarked, $125-150.

MC/S: country unkn, c. 1870-1880, HP and decal, applied MG, $125-150.

Square, demitasse MC/S: country unkn, c. 1860-1870, ribbon handled, four-footed, applied MG, unmarked, $350-375.

MG: recessed and in corner, preceding MC.

MC/S: country unkn, c. 1875-1885, HP, rare pineapple dsn, applied MG, unmarked, $180-240.

MC/S: Germany, c. 1891-1900, HP, rare tree dsn, applied MG, Mark 27, $295-310.

MG: continuation of tree dsn, preceding MC.

MM/S: country unkn, c. 1880-1890, HP, rare blown out stag dsn, applied MG, unmarked, $225-250.

MC/S: Germany, c. 1882-1900, HP and decals, modified pedestal, applied MG, Mark 85, $125-140.

MC/S: country unkn, c. 1883-1889, HP raised and elaborate dsn, applied MG, unmarked, $150-175.

MC/S: country unkn, c. 1878-1888, HP wheat dsn, applied MG, unmarked, $120-130.

MC/S: country unkn, c. 1870-1875, HP and decals, holly berry dsn, rare molded, recessed MG, unmarked, $175-200.

MC/S: country unkn, c. 1875-1885, HP, recessed, applied MG, unmarked, $165-175.

Rare square MC/S: country unkn, c. 1865-1875, HP, rare "tea and toast," unique mold dsn, four half-circle feet, applied MG, unmarked, $450-550.

MC/S: England, c. 1876, HP, unusual bamboo and exotic bird dsn, bamboo handle, applied MG, Mark 28, $275-300.

MC/S: Germany, c. 1892-1899, HP cobalt w/raised gold words, "A Present," applied cobalt MG, Mark 107, $240-260.

MC/S: France, c. 1900-1914, HP and decals, twisted handle, applied MG, Mark 29, $250-300.

MC/S: country unkn, c. 1880-1890, HP, unmatched saucer, applied MG, unmarked, $60-85.

MC/S: France, c. 1904-1920, HP and transfer, sgn "A.C.," applied MG, Mark 38, $300-325.

MC/S: country unkn, c. 1878-1888, HP, applied MG, unmarked, $130-150.

MC/S: country unkn, c. 1875-1885, HP, peach inside cup, unusual mold dsn, applied MG, unmarked, $150-160.

MC/S: France, c. 1891-1914, HP gold and transfer dsn, wishbone handle, applied MG, Mark 30, $300-325.

MC/S: England, c. 1920+, HP exotic plumed birds of paradise dsn, applied MG, Mark 31, $200-225.

MC/S: country unkn, c. 1875-1885, HP swirl dsn mold, modified bamboo handle, applied MG, unmarked, $200-225.

MC/S: Germany, c. 1865-1875, HP, thunderjug shape, footed pedestal, beaded handle, applied MG, Mark 33, $235-250.

MC/S: Germany, c. 1891-1900, HP to mold, applied MG, Mark 33, $225-250.

MG: gold HP dsn, bull's-eye dsn bottom of cup, preceding MC.

MC/S: England, c. 1891-1900, HP exotic flowers and plumed birds of paradise, HP handle, applied MG, Mark 32, $650-750.

MG: HP flowers, preceding MC.

MC/S: France, c. 1894, matte finish, modified swirl mold, sgn and dated, " C. Rae, 1894," applied MG, Mark 19, $375-400.

MC/S: country unkn, c. 1871-1891, rare HP all cobalt and gold, applied gold MG, unmarked, $250-275.

MC/S: country unkn, c. 1870-1880, HP, much wear, open butterfly handle, applied MG, unmarked, $125-175.

MC/S: France, c. 1896-1900, HP, raised gold dsn, applied MG, mark 34, $325-375.

MC/S: Italy, c. unkn, HP, rare Capo-di-Monte style, applied MG, Mark 35, $250-300.

MC/S: England, c. 1892-1899, transfer pattern dsn, half-scissors handle, applied MG, Mark 36, $400-425.

MG: pattern dsn, preceding MC.

MC/S: Germany, c. 1880-1890, HP inside and outside of cup, MG, and saucer, applied MG, Mark 37, $300-325.

MC/S: country unkn, c. 1868-1878, HP to mold, half-scissors handle, small repair to saucer, applied MG, unmarked, $125-175.

MC/S: country unkn, c. 1875-1885, rare HP stylized animal dsn, applied MG, unmarked, $150-175.

MC/S: country unkn, c. 1870-1880, HP raised and applied dsn, deep saucer, applied MG, unmarked, $200-225.

MC/S: France, c. 1904-1920, HP and transfer, footed pedestal, applied MG, Mark 38, $375-400.

MC/S, France, c. 1891-1900, HP, sgn, "M. E.," applied MG, Mark 56, $325-345.

MG: HP yellow, preceding MC.

MC/S: France, c. 1890-1899, HP, brushed matte gold, applied MG, Mark 61, $270-300.

MC/S: country unkn, c. 1870-1880, HP flowers, impressed "Present," applied MG, unmarked, $90-110.

MC/S: Germany, c. 1887-1902, HP and decals, applied MG, Mark 39, $70-90.

MC/S: country unkn, c. 1880-1890, HP and decals, applied MG, unmarked, $70-80.

MC/S: country unkn, c. 1875-1885, HP to mold, cutwork pedestal, applied MG, unmarked, $195-220.

MC/S: France, c. 1870-1885, HP, exotic raised dsn, deep saucer, applied MG, Mark 40, $375-400.

MC/S: country unkn, c. 1875-1885, HP creative dsn, wear, applied MG, unmarked, $75-125.

MC/S: country unkn, c. 1870-1880, HP to raised mold, pedestal, wear, applied MG, unmarked, $85-130.

MC/S: country unknown, c. 1878-1888, HP to blown out dsn, footed pedestal, applied MG, unmarked, $125-135.

MC/S: country unkn, c. 1868-1878, HP icicle dsn, rare molded MG, unmarked, $250-275.

MC/S: France, c. 1893, HP, deep saucer, applied MG, Marks I, 41, $295-310.

MG: HP floral dsn, preceding MC.

MC/S: Germany, c. 1891-1900, HP, unusual dsn, bamboo style handle, applied MG, Mark 42, $200-225.

MG: HP dsn, recessed, preceding MC.

MC/S: country unkn, c. 1874-1884, HP blackberry dsn, applied MG, unmarked, $110-125.

Kettle MC/S: country unkn, c. 1867, HP blown out and applied dsn, four-footed, applied MG, unmarked, $220-240.

MC/S: England or USA, c. 1865-1875, rare HP Majolica, lavender inside cup and center of saucer, twisted rope handle, applied lavender MG, unmarked, $750-850,

MC/S: England, c. 1882, transfer dsn, modified bamboo handle, deep saucer, applied MG, Mark 43, $425-475.

MG: recessed, pattern dsn, preceding MC.

MC/S: country unkn, c. 1875-1885, HP, brandy snifter shape, pedestal, applied MG, unmarked, $135-155.

MC/S: country unkn, c. 1874-1884, HP and transfer, applied MG, unmarked, $150-165.

MC/S: Germany, c. 1887-1897, HP, raised dsn, deep pink lustre, deep saucer, applied MG, Mark 45, $135-145.

MC/S: Oriental, country unkn, c. pre 1891, HP over stencil, applied MG, Mark 44, $300-325.

MC/S: Oriental, country unkn, c. 1850-1890, HP dsn with Foo dogs, applied MG, mark unreadable, $395-425.

Demitasse MC/S: country unkn, c. 1880-1890, HP, raised dsn, four-footed, cutwork on saucer, applied MG, unmarked, $175-200.

MG: HP gold, wear, preceding MC.

MC/S: France, c. 1893-1903, elegant HP dsn, spiderweb on saucer, dsn on handle, sgn, applied MG, Mark 46, $375-400.

MG: HP and scalloped, preceding MC.

MC/S: country unkn, c. 1870-1880, HP, raised and applied lilies of valley, applied MG, unmarked, $200-225.

MC/S: Japan, c. 1891-1921, HP and beading, applied MG, Mark 47, $300-350.

MG: HP and beading, preceding MC.

MC/S: country unkn, c. 1870-1880, HP, primitive dsn, deep saucer, applied MG, unmarked, $110-120.

Demitasse MC/S: country unkn, c. 1875-1885, HP, molded flower handle, applied MG, marked with a raised white cross (possibly old R.S. Prussia), $375-425.

MC/S: Japan, c. 1885-1890, HP and beading, applied MG, unmarked (Gaudy Nippon), $225-250.

MG: decorated, beaded, preceding MC.

MC/S: France, c. 1906, HP, sgn and dated, applied MG, Mark 19, $275-300.

MG: HP rose dsn, preceding MC.

Sgn: gold, on saucer, preceding MC/S.

MC/S: USA, c. 1949+, HP, matte gold, recessed and applied MG, Marks 8, 65, $85-95.

MC/S: country unkn, c. 1880-1890, HP, rare molded and raised MG, unmarked, $200-250.

MC/S: Germany, c. 1880-1910, HP lustre, four-footed, applied MG, Mark 48 (rare R.S. Prussia), $500-525.

MC/S: country unkn, c. 1875-1885, HP over swirl mold, applied MG, unmarked, $150-175.

MC/S: country unkn, c. 1877-1887, HP to unusual mold, modified bamboo handle, applied MG, unmarked, $190-210.

MC/S: France, c. 1891, sgn and dated, HP matte gold, rare handle dsn, applied MG, Mark 19, $290-300.

Handle: rare, twisted dsn, preceding MC.

MC/S France, c. 1896-1900, HP and transfer, deep saucer, applied MG, Mark 49, $245-265.

MC/S: Germany, c. 1891-1901, HP, rare molded MG, marked, "Made in Germany," $200-225.

MC/S: country unkn, c. 1875-1885, undecorated (possibly Limoges whiteware), applied MG, unmarked, $90-100.

MC/S: country unkn, c. pre-1891, no dsn, applied MG, unmarked, $100-125.

MC/S: France, c. 1893-1903, HP, desired pansy dsn, scalloped, rare twisted handle, applied MG, Marks 46, 50, $350-375.

MC/S: Germany, c. 1901-1910, HP dainty dsn, applied MG, Mark 51, $250-275.

Octagon MC/S: country unkn, c. 1880-1890, HP w/applied gold, braided handle, applied recessed MG, mark unreadable, $135-145.

Hexagon MC/S: Germany, c. 1900, transfer dsn, applied MG, Mark 52, $135-145.

MC/S: France, c. 1855-1875, HP over swirled mold, applied MG, Mark 53, $335-355.

MC/S: country unkn, c. 1880-1890, HP to mold dsn, applied MG, unmarked, $150-170.

MC/S: Japan, c. 1906-1916, HP, much gold and cobalt, unmatched saucer, applied MG, Mark 54, $200-250.

MC/S: country unkn, c. 1870-1880, HP intricate dsn, applied raised MG, unmarked, $175-200.

Demitasse MC/S: France, c. 1890-1899, HP, flakes and repair, applied MG, Mark 6I, $100-240.

MC/S: England, c. 1868-1883, rare, HP Majolica, bird on fan, lavender inside, chips, applied MG, impressed English registry mark, $490-600.

MG: HP, brushed gold, preceding MC/S.

MC/S: France, c. 1876-1900, transfer Princess pattern, deep saucer, applied MG, Mark 55, $210-240.

MC/S: Germany, c. 1902, transfer dsn, applied MG, Mark 10, $120-130.

MC/S: Oriental, country unkn, c. 1880-1890, HP, unmatched saucer, applied MG, unmarked, $80-130.

Interior MC: HP bull's-eye dsn, preceding MC.

MC/S: country unkn, c. 1880-1890, HP, four-footed, applied MG, unmarked, $160-175.

MC/S: Austria, c. 1891-1918, HP, deep saucer, applied MG, Mark 57, $150-160.

MC/S: France, c. 1881-1885, HP, applied MG, Mark 56, $175-200.

MC/S: country unkn, c. 1870-1880, pres, "Think of Me," applied MG, unmarked, $95-110.

MC/S: country unkn, c. 1880-1890, HP, applied MG, unmarked, $95-110.

MC/S: country unkn, c. 1875-1885, HP, pedestal, unusual, applied MG, unmarked, $115-125.

MC/S: Austria, c. 1891-1918, transfer dsn, chip, applied MG, Mark 57, $45-120.

MM/S: country unkn, c. 1875-1885, HP and transfer, rare molded MG, unmarked, $260-270.

MG: raised and molded, preceding MC.

MC/S: country unkn, c. 1878-1888, HP, very unusual lustres and applied dsn, applied MG, unmarked, $150-175.

MC/S: country unkn, c. 1880-1890, HP and applied dsn, applied MG, unmarked, $125-135.

Kettle MC/S: country unkn, c. 1875-1885, HP, applied dsn, gold beading, footed pedestal, applied MG, unmarked, $145-155.

MC/S: Germany, c. 1873-1883, HP w/applied dsn, applied MG, marked, "Germany," in a circle, $140-160.

MC/S: France, c. 1855-1875, HP, swirled and scalloped, applied MG, Marks 53, 58, $300-320.

MC/S: country unkn, c. 1878-1888, HP, applied gold and cobalt dsn, interior cup gold, applied MG, unmarked, $155-170.

MC/S: Austria, c. 1891-1918, HP icicle dsn, applied MG, Mark 59, $225-250.

MC/S: country unkn, c. 1880-1890, HP, applied dsn, applied MG, unmarked, $150-160.

MC/S: country unkn, c. 1880-1890, HP, applied gold, four-footed, applied MG, unmarked, $175-195.

Farmer's MC/S: England, c. 1856-1862, HP, "Japanese" dsn, applied MG, marked, "C & H (Cockson & Harding, Staffordshire, England), Japanese (pattern)," $900-1,000.

Square MC/S: country unkn, c. 1870-1880, HP, swirled mold, applied MG, unmarked, $175-200.

MC/S: country unkn, c. 1875-1885, HP and transfer dsn, four-footed, wear, applied MG, unmarked, $115-120.

MC/S: country unkn, c. 1870-1880, HP to mold, applied MG, unmarked, $200-220.

MC/S: Japan, c. 1891-1918, HP, very ornate, beading, applied MG, Mark 60, $435-455.

Kettle MC/S: country unkn, c. 1880-1890, HP spongeware, applied dsn, four-footed, rope handle, applied MG, unmarked, $300-325.

MG: HP, ornate dsn, preceding MC.

MC/S: country unkn, c. 1880-1890, HP acorn dsn, sgn "Burkel," applied MG, unmarked, $250-275.

MC/S: country unkn, c. 1880-1890, transfer dsn, four-footed, deep saucer, applied MG, unmarked, $90-95.

MC/S: France, c. 1890-1899, HP, gold sponge dsn, applied MG, Mark 61, $300-310.

MG: gold sponge dsn, preceding MC.

MC/S: country unkn, c. 1875-1885, HP, saucer cracked, applied MG, unmarked, $110-150.

MC/S: German, c. 1891-1910, HP and decal, applied MG, Mark 62, $120-130.

MC/S: country unkn, c. 1880-1885, HP, deep saucer, applied MG, unmarked, $110-120.

Square MC/S: England, c. 1885, decals, unusual saucer dsn, applied MG in corner of cup, Mark 63, $225-235.

MC/S: England, c. 1868-1883, rare HP Majolica, floral handle, applied purple MG, marked with English registry mark (partly indistinct), $800-900.

MC/S: Ireland, c. 1891-1926, HP shamrocks, lustre, and basket weave dsn, split twig handle, applied MG, Mark 117 (second black mark), $1,100-1,300.

MC/S: German, c. 1891-1900, HP and transfer, wear, applied MG, Mark 64, $90-130.

MC/S: Germany, c. 1891-1920, transfer dsn, unmatched saucer, applied MG, Mark 118, $85-90.

MC/S: country unkn, c. 1875-1885, HP and decal, chip, wear, applied MG, unmarked, $50-115.

MC/S: country unkn, c. 1880-1890, HP, unusual dsn over swirl mold, applied MG, unmarked, $175-195.

MG: unusual scalloped dsn, preceding MC.

MC/S: Oriental, country unkn, c. pre 1891, HP, intricate gold dsn, applied MG, marked with Oriental characters, $300-325.

MC/S: country unkn, c. 1880-1891, HP, lustre, applied MG, unmarked, $90-100.

MC/S: country unkn, c. 1875-1885, HP and brushed gold, half-scissors handle, applied MG, unmarked, $170-180.

Left-handed MC/S: country unkn, c. 1880-1890, copper lustre and transfer, applied MG, unmarked, $550-600.

Left-handed MC/S: Austria, 1892+, HP, rare cherry dsn, applied MG, marked "Austria," $450-500.

Left-handed MC/S: country unkn, c. unkn—reproduction, HP and transfer, applied MG, unmarked fake.

Left-handed MC/S: country unkn, c. 1880-1890, transfer dsn, applied MG, unmarked, $700-750.

Left-handed MC/S: country unkn, c. unkn—reproduction, HP and transfer, applied MG, unmarked fake.

Left-handed MC/S: country unkn, c. 1880-1890, HP and transfer, rare fruit and nut dsn, applied MG, unmarked, $800-900.

MC/S: country unkn, c. 1870-1880, pres, HP and transfer, some wear, applied MG, unmarked, $90-100.

MC/S: country unkn, c. 1875-1885, pres, HP, deep saucer, applied MG, unmarked, $175-185.

MC/S: country unkn, c. 1875-1885, pres, HP to mold, applied MG, unmarked, $120-150.

MC/S: Germany, c. 1875-1880, pres, HP, applied decoration, message in German, "May your fortunes blossom," applied MG, unmarked, $175-185.

MC/S: country unkn, c. 1875-1885, pres, HP, lustre, applied MG, unmarked, $175-200.

MC/S: Germany, c. 1875-1885, pres, HP and transfer, message in German, "This cup is for anyone who can twist his mustache," pedestal, applied MG, unmarked, $170-190.

MC/S: Germany, c. 1887-1897, pres, "Brother" (rare), HP and transfer dsn, applied MG, Mark 45, $170-190.

Farmers' MC/S: Germany, c. 1875-1885, pres, HP and transfer, applied MG, Mark 90, $155-165.

MC/S: Germany, c. 1887-1897, pres, HP, lustre, applied decoration, applied MG, Mark 45, $200-210.

MC/S: country unkn, c. 1879, pres, HP, personalized and dated, slight wear on gold, applied MG, unmarked, $200-225.

MC/S: Germany, c. 1880-1890, pres, transfer dsn, message in German, "To protect your pretty mustache, this cup has an edge to it," applied MG, unmarked, $165-175.

MC/S: country unkn, c. 1875-1885, pres, HP, gold lustre, personalized, "Adam Cob," applied MG, unmarked, $225-250.

MC/S: England, c. 1870-1880, pres, transfer w/ Sunderland lustre, applied MG, unmarked, $300-350.

Reverse side: "Sailor's Lament," preceding MC.

MC/S: England, c. 1870-1880, pres, transfer w/ Sunderland lustre, "Sailor's Farewell," on reverse side, applied MG, unmarked, $300-350.

MG: Sunderland lustre dsn, preceding MC.

MC/S: country unkn, c. 1875-1885, pres, HP and decal, applied MG, unmarked, $150-165.

MC/S: country unkn, c. 1880-1890, pres, HP raised dsn and lustre, applied MG, unmarked, $170-185.

MC/S: England, c. 1913-1930, rare adv transfer, applied MG, Mark 66, $175-200.

MC/S: Germany, c. 1891-1900, pres, HP, applied MG, Mark 42, $150-160.

MC/S: country unkn, c. 1875-1885, port, HP and decal, applied MG, unmarked, $275-300.

MC/S: England, c. 1895-1896, com, Queen Victoria's Jubilee, HP and transfer, floral handle, applied MG, Mark 67, $300-350.

MC/S: country unkn, c. 1878-1888, rare inset port, HP and decal, applied MG, unmarked, $250-275.

MC/S: Germany, c. 1891-1910, port, HP cobalt and gold, decal, applied MG, Marks 62, 68, $215-225.

MC/S: country unkn, c. 1870-1880, cameo, Greek Key dsn, rare molded MG, unmarked, $300-350.

MG: raised and molded, Greek Key dsn, preceding MC.

Demitasse MC/S: country unkn, c. 1880-1890, fig, HP and decal, modified bamboo handle, wear, applied MG, unmarked, $100-175.

Demitasse MC/S: Germany, c. 1883-1893, fig, HP and decal, applied MG, Mark 69, $350-375.

MC/S: Germany, c. 1891-1910, fig, HP and decal, applied MG, Mark 70, $170-180.

MC/S: Germany, c. 1885-1895, fig, HP and decal, applied MG, marked "Royal Bavaria," $160-175.

Rare miniature MC/S: Germany, c. 1892-1910, souv, transfer and gold, rare molded MG, marked, "Made in Germany for Dover, New Jersey," $400-450.

MC/S: country unkn, c. 1875-1885, fig, HP and rare cherubs decal, applied MG, unmarked, $200-225.

MC/S: Oriental, country unkn, c. 1880-1890, HP over stencil, unmatched saucer (hard to detect), applied MG, unmarked, $225-245.

MG: HP ornate dsn, preceding MC.

MC/S: Oriental, country unkn, c. 1880-1890, HP, possibly over stencil, applied MG, marked in Oriental characters, $250-275.

MC/S: Oriental, country unkn, c. pre 1891, HP Oriental dsn, lustre, applied MG, Mark 71, $275-300.

MG: Oriental dsn, lustre, preceding MC.

MC/S: Germany, c. 1891-1910, souv, transfer, much wear, applied MG, Mark 72, $50-100.

MC/S: country unkn, c. 1880-1890, souv, transfer and gold spatter, applied MG, unmarked, $90-100.

MC/S: Germany, c. 1918-1925, souv, transfer and gold, applied MG, Mark 73, $90-100.

MC/S: country unkn, c. 1891-1910, souv, transfer and HP, applied MG, Mark 74, $100-115.

MC/S: England, c. 1871-1891, souv, transfer (Statue of Faith, and *Mayflower*), unusual handle, applied MG, Mark 75, $225-250.

MC/S: Germany, c. 1891-1910, souv, transfer, wear, applied MG, Mark 76, $100-120.

MC/S: country unkn, c. 1880-1890, souv, HP, lustre and gold, raised dsn, applied MG, unmarked, $170-180.

MC/S: Germany, c. 1891-1910, souv, transfer, wear, applied MG, Mark 77, $100-120.

MC/S: country unkn, c. 1890-1900, souv, transfer (Ontario, Canada), applied MG, unmarked, $120-130.

MC/S: Germany, c. 1891-1910, souv, transfer, very visible old repair, applied MG, Mark 78, $20-100.

MC/S: England, c. 1891-1904, souv, transfer, applied MG, Mark 79, $250-275.

Chapter Two

Ceramic Mustache Cups Sans Saucers

Chapter Two presents those ceramic mustache cups and mugs that were acquired without saucers. Most of the cups originally came with matching saucers, but over the years these were misplaced or broken. Although serious collectors prefer a cup with matching saucer, they will not reject a single cup if it is attractive and intact. Chips, hairlines, flakes, cracks, and repairs diminish the artistic as well as the monetary value of mustache cups.

There are exceptions of course. For example, Victorian Majolica, being earthenware, is easily damaged. It is also scarce and highly desirable, especially if lined in lavender. A collector or dealer would not necessarily reject such a mustache cup with good repairs, small chips, or flakes.

A few cups and most stein-like mugs probably never had saucers. Although some of the rare kettle-shaped cups with their delicate feet are found with matching saucers, we suspect the larger ones never did have saucers. They may have had tiny cup plates only. The stein-like mugs, as with most steins, did not. A good number of single cups or mugs do have a mark or backstamp. Captions appearing with each of those pictured will direct you to the mark in Chapter Six.

Although cups with saucers are highly desirable, cups sans saucers take up less room in a display cabinet, a good reason for including them in a collection. Also, more single cups are to be found in today's scarce market than a matched set. And of course, a saucer is a saucer, but a mustache cup with its unique mustache guard is a collectible!

MM: Germany, c. 1870-1880, HP, rare cherub handle (not shown), applied MG, unmarked, $150-175.

MC: USA, c. 1880-1890, HP, "Old Man of the Mountain," New Hampshire, applied MG, unmarked, $85-100.

MC: country unkn, c. 1880-1890, transfer dsn w/HP gold spatter, applied MG, unmarked, $75-85.

MC: Germany, c. 1901-1910, HP, unusual shape, applied MG, Mark 51, $110-150.

MC: USA/England, c. 1870-1880, rare HP Majolica, flakes, applied MG, unmarked, $325-350.

Rare seashell MC: country unkn, c. 1880-1890, HP, wishbone handle, four-footed, applied MG, unmarked, $145-175.

MC: country unkn, c. 1880-1890, HP and decal, applied MG, unmarked, $70-90.

MC: country unkn, c. 1865-1875, HP, matte finish, rare fan handle, repair to cup, applied MG, unmarked, $65-175.

MC: country unkn, c. 1880-1890, HP, bamboo handle (not shown), applied MG, unmarked, $100-125.

MC: country unkn, c. 1870-1880, HP, rare raised and molded MG, unmarked, $160-180.

MC: country unkn, c. 1886, HP, unusual boxcar handle, sgn, applied MG, unmarked, $175-200.

Sgn: "L.E.E., Xmas, '86," gold, preceding MC.

Kettle MC: country unkn, c. 1880-1890, HP, four-footed, applied MG, unmarked, $135-155.

MC: Oriental, country unkn, c. 1875-1885, HP, beading, applied MG, unmarked, $110-120.

MG: raised and decorated, preceding MC.

MC: Germany, c. 1891-1900, HP, raised gold, applied MG, Mark 107, $100-125.

Demitasse MC: country unkn, c. 1850-1860, HP, unusual shape, unusual latch dsn handle, applied MG, unmarked, $125-145.

MC: Germany, c. 1891-1910, HP and decal, applied MG, Mark 80, $70-90.

MC: country unkn, c. 1845-1855, copper lustre, raised dsn, early piece, four-footed, applied MG, unmarked, $170-190.

MC: country unkn, c. 1870-1880, HP and decal, half-scissors handle, applied MG, unmarked, $60-75.

MC: country unkn, c. 1880-1890, HP, applied MG, unmarked, $95-110.

MC: country unkn, c. 1870-1880, HP to mold dsn, applied MG, unmarked, $115-125.

MC: Germany, c. 1918-1920, HP outside and inside, scalloped rims, unusual shape, applied MG, Marks 73, 81, $125-145.

MC: country unkn, c. 1880-1890, HP over swirl mold, unmarked, applied MG, $120-140.

MC: Germany, c. 1890, HP and decal, lustre, applied MG, Mark 82, $110-120.

MC: France, c. 1881-1885, HP, applied MG, Mark 84, $145-155.

MC: France, c. 1889-1905, HP outside and inside, applied MG, Mark 83, $135-150.

MG: HP decoration, preceding MC.

Kettle MC: country unkn, c. 1870-1880, HP, lustre, blown out and applied gold dsn, four-footed, applied MG, unmarked, $155-165.

MC: country unkn, c. 1880-1890, decal dsn, much wear, applied MG, unmarked, $35-75.

MC: country unkn, c. 1880-1890, HP, lustre and gold, small chip on gold, applied MG, unmarked, $65-125.

Kettle MC: country unkn, c. 1870-1880, HP cobalt and gold, blown out, applied MG, four-footed, unmarked, $160-170.

MC: country unkn, c. 1870-1880, HP dsn in relief, applied MG, unmarked, $135-155.

Oval MC: country unkn, c. 1880-1890, HP exotic floral dsn w/ desirable pink interior, applied MG, unmarked, $165-185.

MC: country unkn, c. 1870-1880, HP, rare raised, molded MG, unmarked, $140-160.

Kettle MC: country unkn, c. 1870-1880, HP cobalt and elaborate applied dsn, four-footed, applied MG, unmarked, $200-225.

MC: Germany, c. 1882-1900, decal dsn, applied MG, Mark 85, $90-110.

MC: country unkn, c. 1885-1891, HP, applied MG, unmarked, $85-100.

MC: country unkn, c. 1880-1890, unusual HP bird dsn, wear, applied MG, unmarked, $115-125.

MC: Germany, c. 1891-1900, unusual HP fruit dsn, applied MG, marked, "Lichtenstein, Germany," $135-185.

MC: country unkn, c. 1880-1890, transfer winter dsn, applied MG, unmarked, $100-110.

MC: country unkn, c. 1875-1885, unusual snowflake pattern, applied MG, unmarked, $150-180.

MG: unusual snowflake pattern, preceding MC.

Hexagonal MC: Austria, c. 1885-1890, exotic floral dsn, applied MG, Mark 86, $140-160.

MC: country unkn, c. 1880-1890, HP, applied MG, unmarked, $110-120.

MC: country unkn, c. 1880-1890, HP, applied MG, unmarked, $100-110.

MC: England, c. 1887, HP ivy dsn, modified bamboo handle, applied MG, Mark 87, $250-275.

MG: ivy dsn, preceding MG.

MM: country unkn, c. 1870-1880, HP moss rose dsn, rare cherub handle (not shown), applied MG, unmarked, $150-175.

MC: country unkn, c. 1870-1880, HP, question mark handle, applied MG, unmarked, $125-145.

MC: country unkn, c. 1860-1870, HP, applied MG, unmarked, $100-110.

MM: country unkn, c. 1865-1875, HP raised dsn, four-footed, applied MG, unmarked, $125-145.

MC: country unkn, c. 1870-1880, HP moss rose and beading, applied MG, unmarked, $115-125.

MC: country unkn, c. pre-1891, Oriental dsn, applied MG, blue mark unkn, $135-145.

MC: Japan, c. 1890-1921, HP, applied MG, Marks 11, 88, $140-150.

MG: HP floral dsn, preceding MC.

Seashell MC: country unkn, c. 1880-1890, HP, wishbone handle, four-footed, applied MG, unmarked, $135-150.

MG: HP decoration, preceding MC.

MC: country unkn, c. 1850-1860, HP, applied MG, unmarked, $110-115.

Octagonal MC: country unkn, c. 1870-1880, HP castle scenes, applied MG, box handle, unmarked, $140-165.

MC: France, c. 1890-1910, HP, scalloped rims, applied MG, Mark 89, $130-150.

MC: country unkn, c. 1880-1891, HP, some wear, applied MG, unmarked, $65-90.

MC: country unkn, c. 1870-1880, HP, lustre and raised gold dsn, applied MG, unmarked, $120-130.

MG: HP floral decoration, preceding MC.

MC: country unkn, c. 1885-1891, decal dsn, applied MG, unmarked, $70-75.

Kettle MC: country unkn, c. 1860-1870, HP and applied lace underglaze, unusual flower and stem handle, four-footed, applied MG, unmarked, $175-200.

MC: country unkn, c. 1880-1890, decal, applied MG, unmarked, $50-55.

MC: country unkn, c. 1880-1891, decal ribbon dsn, applied MG, unmarked, $65-75.

MM: country unkn, c. 1875-1880, rare HP pansies, applied MG, unmarked, $125-145.

MC: country unkn, c. 1880-1890, HP, applied MG, unmarked, $100-110.

Farmer's MC: country unkn, c. 1880-1890, HP, pink lustre, applied MG, unmarked, $125-150.

MC: Germany, c. 1875-1885, transfer dsn, applied MG, Mark 90, $110-120.

Demitasse MC: France 1890-1899, HP, applied MG, Mark 61, $140-160.

MC: country unkn, c. 1880-1890, HP, cobalt and gold w/bird and butterfly dsn, gold touch-up, applied MG, unmarked, $95-150.

MC: country unkn, c. 1860-1870, HP, rare aqua and lavender lustre w/raised gold, applied MG, unmarked, $160-190.

MC: England, c. 1968+, Flow Blue dsn, blue handle, applied MG, marked, "Ironstone Staffordshire, England," $110-120.

Kettle MC: country unkn, c. 1870-1880, HP, cobalt w/ raised gold, four-footed, wear on gold, applied MG, unmarked, $125-145.

MC: France, c. 1867, HP violets (desirable), applied MG, marked, "France," $125-145.

MG: HP gold dsn, preceding MC.

MC: Oriental, country unkn, c. 1880-1890, HP, paneled cobalt and floral dsn, applied MG, unmarked, $110-120.

MC: country unkn, c. 1870-1880, HP unique dsn, applied MG, unmarked, $120-130.

Demitasse MC: Germany, c. 1887-1902, HP, applied MG, Mark 91, $135-145.

MC: Germany, c. 1880-1910, HP, applied MG, Marks 48, 92, $250-275.

MC: country unkn, c. 1880-1890, HP spatter dsn, applied MG, unmarked, $ 110-120.

Demitasse MC: Germany, c. 1915-1925, HP, applied MG, Mark, "R.S. Germany," (green wreath mark), $150-175.

MC: country unkn, c. 1870-1890, HP and transfer dsn, applied MG, unmarked, $90-100.

MC: country unkn, c. 1885-1890, HP, swirled mold, applied MG, unmarked, $115-125.

Modified kettle MC: country unkn, c. 1875-1880, HP, very rare three-footed, applied MG, unmarked, $350-375.

Demitasse MC: Germany, c. 1887-1902, HP, applied MG, Mark 25, $135-145.

MC: country unkn, c. 1885-1890, HP, applied MG, unmarked, $120-130.

Left-handed MC: country unkn, c. 1865-1875, HP and rare decal, applied MG, unmarked, $325-350.

Left-handed MC: country unkn, c. 1865-1875, HP and rare decal, wear, applied MG, unmarked, $300-325.

Left-handed MC: country unkn, c. unkn—reproduction, HP and decal, applied MG, Mark 94—fake R.S. Prussia mark.

MC: country unkn, c. 1880-1890, pres, HP, applied MG, unmarked, $100-110.

MM: country unkn, c. 1885-1890, pres, HP cobalt and raised gold, rare cherub handle, applied MG, unmarked, $250-300.

Rare handle: cherub dsn, preceding MM.

MC: country unkn, c. 1880-1890, pres, HP, lustre and raised gold, applied MG, unmarked, $130-140.

MM: country unkn, c. 1885-1890, pres, HP, cobalt and raised gold, cherub handle, applied MG, unmarked, $220-240.

Rare handle: cherub dsn, preceding MM.

MC: country unkn, c. 1880-1890, pres, HP, much wear, applied MG, unmarked, $70-115.

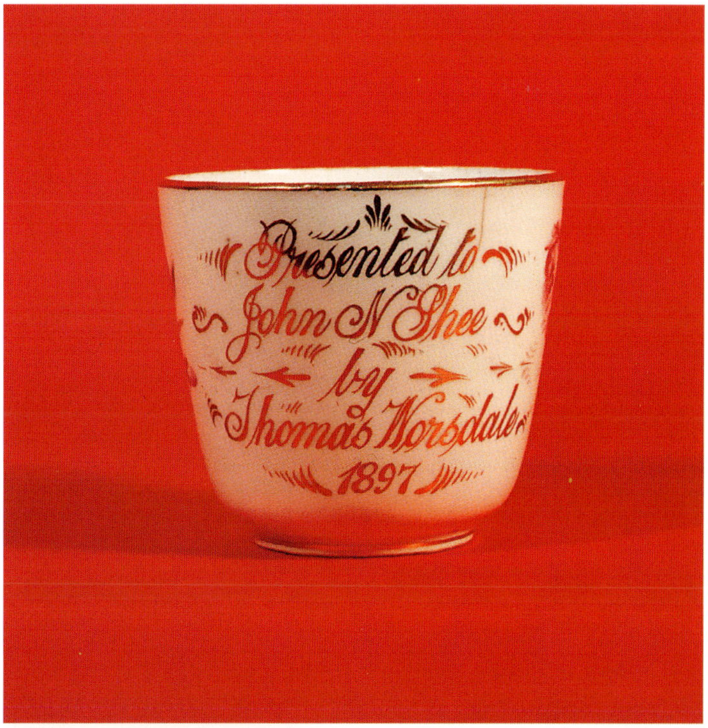

MC: country unkn, c. 1897, pres, HP, applied MG, unmarked, $120-130.

MC: country unkn, c. 1885-1890, pres, HP, unusual cobalt handle, applied MG, unmarked, $125-150.

Cobalt handle: preceding MC.

MM: country unkn, c. 1880-1890, pres, HP, much wear, rare cherub handle, applied MG, unmarked, $100-190.

Rare handle: cherub dsn, preceding MM.

MM: country unkn, c. 1885-1890, pres, HP raised dsn, applied MG, unmarked, $120-130.

MC: country unkn, c. 1880-1890, pres, HP, wear, applied MG, unmarked, $80-115.

MM: Germany, c. 1880-1890, pres, HP, much wear, applied MG, Mark 45 in red, $65-115.

MC: country unkn, c. 1875-1885, pres, HP, pearlescent lustre, applied MG, unmarked, $135-145.

MC: country unkn, c. 1870-1880, pres, HP, applied MG, unmarked, $125-135.

MC: Germany, c. 1880-1890, pres, HP, wear, twisted rope handle, applied MG, Mark 45, $110-120.

Oval MC: Germany, c. 1865-1875, pres, HP, message in German, applied MG, unmarked, $145-165.

MC: Germany, c. 1892-1910, pres, applied MG, Mark 107, $95-100.

MC: country unkn, c. 1870-1875, pres, HP raised dsn, lustre and gold, applied MG, unmarked, $140-150.

MC: country unkn, c. 1870-1880, pres, HP, lustre and raised dsn, applied MG, unmarked, $130-140.

Left:
MC: Germany, c. 1865-1875, pres, HP, applied MG, Mark 107, $100-120.

Right:
MC: country unkn, c. 1860-1870, HP and decal scenic dsn, applied MG, unmarked, $110-120.

MC: England, c. 1902, com, HP, pink lustre and coronation decal of Queen Alexandra and King Edward VII, 1902, applied MG, unmarked, $225-250.

MC: Germany, c. unknown, port, decal of Napoleon, applied MG, Mark 95, $250-275.

Left:
MC: country unkn, c. 1865-1875, port, rare decal of four little girls, applied MG, unmarked, $250-275.

Right:
MC: country unkn, c. 1865-1875, fig, decal of cherubs, applied MG, unmarked, $l50-160.

MC: country unkn, c. 1880-1890, fig, HP and decal of two girls and a goat, applied MG, unmarked, $170-190.

MC: Germany, c. 1891-1910, fig, HP and decal of bathers in stream, applied MG, Mark 62, $150-175.

Kettle MC: country unkn, c. 1875-1885, fig, HP spongeware and decal of man and woman with dogs, unusual handle, four-footed, applied MG, unmarked, $200-225.

Rare handle: preceding MC.

Demitasse MC: country unkn, c. 1891-1900, fig, HP and decals in ovals, applied MG, Mark 96, $200-225.

Figural MC: reverse side of preceding MC.

MG: HP gold dsn, preceding MC.

Chapter Three

SILVER MUSTACHE CUPS

If "a good man nowadays is hard to find," as an old song laments, then a good silver mustache cup is harder. For every hundred ceramic cups found, one is lucky to find even one silver cup.

All of the silver cups pictured in this book are silverplated. No sterling silver mustache cup has ever been seen by these collectors. All of the cups pictured were manufactured in the United States. None were found from any other country.

As with all silverplated items, mustache cups are subject to wear. The condition of the pictured cups ranges from excellent to much wear. The wear occurs from use, washing, and polishing. Replating the cups is not usually advised. It will probably cost more than you paid for the cup, and further erosion of the decoration is possible.

Silverplated mustache cups are sought after diligently by serious collectors. Fortunately, almost all of these cups are well marked, a plus in determining their value. Some silverplated cups were found with mismatched saucers or no saucers at all. What happened to the original saucers? We can assume they didn't crack or break, so we must presume that they were lost.

Mustache cups reached their peak of popularity in the United States around the time of The Gold Rush. No mention of solid gold cups or cups decorated with gold nuggets has turned up during our research, but silver cups lined in gold were found to exist. This co-author has only one in her collection. Which do you think is more highly prized—a gold lining or a silver one? The answer is gold, of course, because it is more valuable and therefore rarer. Another old song rejoices "every cloud must have a silver lining —." So, you can be a happy collector if you find a silverplated cup with either a gold or a silver lining and you can afford it without starving for a week!

SMC/S: USA, c. 1880-1890, engraved dsn, pedestled C/S, scalloped MG, Mark 3-S, $300-325.

Marks on Silver Mustache Cups

Since the markings on silverplated mustache cups are quite different from those found on ceramic cups, they are being treated in this chapter, rather than Chapter Six. These marks are etched/incised on the bottom of the cups and/ or saucers. As the few symbols found on the cups are very basic, such as a "P" in a diamond shape, they will be described rather than drawn. Photographing them was impossible due to lighting and reflection as well as the small size.

Mark 1-S: Pairpoint Mfg. Co., quadruple plate, symbol: "P" in a diamond shape.
Mark 2-S: Meriden Silverplate Co., quadruple plate, symbol: lion holding a goblet.
Mark 3-S: Woodman Cook Co., quadruple plate.
Mark 4-S: Derby Silver Co., Derby, Conn., quadruple plate, symbol: anchor over a crown in a circle.
Mark 5-S: Pairpoint Mfg. Co., New Bedford, Mass., quadruple plate, symbol: "P" in diamond in circle.
Mark 6-S: Rogers & Bro., Patented Sept. 6th, 1887, triple plate.
Mark 7-S: Meriden B, Co., quadruple plate, symbol: scales of justice in a circle.
Mark 8-S: Wilcox Silverplate Co., Meriden, Conn., quadruple plate, symbol: crossed hammers in a circle.
Mark 9-S: Barbour Bros. Co., Silver, quadruple plate.
Mark 10-S: James W. Tufts, Boston, warranted triple plate, quadruple plate.
Mark 11-S: James W. Tufts Co., Silver, warranted quadruple plate.
Mark 12-S: Homan's Silverplate Co., quadruple plate.
Mark 13-S: Victor Silver Co., quadruple plate.
Mark 14-S: Meriden B. Co., quadruple plate, USA, symbol: balance scale.
Mark 15-S: Guaranteed by Roger Smith & Co., Meriden, Conn., USA.

SMC/S: USA, c. 1875-1885, chased dsn, applied MG, Mark 5-S, $350-400.

SMC/S: USA, c. 1870-1880, engraved, French horn handle, pedestled C/S, applied MG, Mark 1-S, $400-425.

SMC/S: USA, c. 1885-1890, engraved dsn, applied MG, Mark 6-S, $400-425.

SMC/S: USA, c. 1869-1874, chased dsn, applied MG, Mark 2-S, $400-425.

SMC/S: USA, c. 1870-1875, raised dsn, monogram on applied MG, Mark 4-S, $400-425.

SMC/S: USA, c. 1870-1880, satin engraved, unmatched saucer, applied MG, mark unreadable, $175-200.

SMC/S: USA, c. 1870-1880, applied rope dsn, thumbprint, raised MG, Mark 8-S, $375-400.

SMC/S: USA, c. 1870-1875, engraved dsn, unmatched saucer, applied MG, Mark 4-S, $225-275.

SMC/S: USA, c. 1870-1880, satin engraved allover dsn, monogram, gold lined, applied MG, Mark 7-S, $450-475.

SMC/S: USA, c. 1870-1880, engraved, unmatched saucer, applied MG, Mark 8-S, $225-275.

SMC/S: country unkn, c. 1870-1880, satin engraved dsn, pedestled saucer, applied MG, unmarked, $275-300.

SMC/S: USA, c. 1880-1890, engraved dsn, pedestled C/S, applied MG, Mark 9-S, $350-375.

SMC/S: USA, c. 1870-1880, undecorated, unmatched saucer, applied MG, Mark 10-S, $150-175.

SMC/S: USA, c. 1870-1880, chased dsn, unmatched saucer, applied MG, Mark 9-S, $250-275.

SMC/S: USA, c. 1880-1890, engraved dsn, initial "F," provenance, applied MG, Mark 11-S, $350-375.

SMC/S: USA, c. 1875-1885, engraved, applied MG, Mark 12-S, $375-400.

SMC/S: USA, c. 1890-1900, etched dsn, beading, much wear, applied MG, Mark 13-S, $175-200.

SMC/S: USA, c. 1875-1885, hammered dsn, unmatched saucer, applied MG, Mark 5-S, $225-250.

SMC/S: USA, c. 1892-1900, swirl dsn, deep saucer, applied MG, Mark 14-S, $425-450.

SMC/S: USA, c. 1880-1890, satin engraved, unmatched saucer, applied MG, Mark 11-S, $225-250.

SMC/S: USA, c. 1875-1885, hammered dsn, unmatched saucer, applied MG, Mark 5-S, $225-250.

Left:
SMC/S: USA, c. 1885-1895, satin engraved, pedestled C/S, applied MG, Mark 1-S, $425-450.

Right:
SMC: USA, c. 1875-1885, engraved, personalized, "To Rev. & Mrs. J. F. Forbes," unusual handle, applied MG, Mark 8-S, $325-350.

SMC: USA, c. 1892-1902, satin engraved, applied rope dsn, scalloped MG, Mark 15-S, $300-350.

Rare PMC: country unkn, c. unkn, engraved, "Papa," soldered handle and MG, marked, "hand-made," $275-300.

Artist's renditions:

SMC: USA, c. 1895, satin engraved, gold lined, applied MG, Meriden Brittania Company, as shown in S.F. Myers' 1895 Catalogue, original cost $12.

SMC: USA, c. 1885, gold lined, applied MG, Reed & Barton, original cost $8.25.

SMC: USA, c. 1895, satin engraved, gold lined, Meriden Brittania Company, as shown in S.F. Myers' 1895 Catalogue, original cost $11.63.

SMC: USA, c. 1885, gold lined, applied MG, Reed & Barton, original cost $6.50.

110 SEARS, ROEBUCK & CO., Cheapest Supply House on Earth, Chicago. CATALOGUE No. 111.

BEST QUADRUPLE PLATED SILVERWARE—CUPS AND NAPKIN RINGS.

THE BEST MONEY CAN BUY. EACH PIECE IS WARRANTED TO BE EXACTLY AS REPRESENTED.

THIS WARE IS QUADRUPLE PLATED with pure silver on genuine Britannia metal. Britannia metal is a white composition metal, same color as silver, hard and durable. It will not corrode and is without question the best metal used in hollow silver plated ware.

SEE THE PRICES WE ARE QUOTING. Examine our designs. If not found the very latest patterns, if our ware is not the very best and the quotations the cheapest of any, don't buy.

No. 5R7119 Child's Cup, bright finished, gold lined, beaded and embossed; height, 2½ inches. Price........$1.75

No. 5R7122 Child's Cup, satin finished, gold lined, hand engraved; height, 3 inches. Price....................$1.50

No. 5R7125 Child's Cup, plain, bright finished, gold lined; height, 3 inches. Price....................$1.40

No. 5R7128 Child's Cup, satin finished, hand engraved, gold lined; height, 3 inches. Price....................$1.40

No. 5R7132 Child's Cup, satin finished, hand engraved, gold lined; height, 3 inches. Price....................$1.35

No. 5R7135 Child's Cup, plain, bright finished, beaded borders, gold lined; height, 2 inches. Price..........$1.30

No. 5R7138 Child's Cup, satin finished, hand engraved, gold lined; height, 2½ inches. Price....................$1.10

No. 5R7140 Child's Cup, satin finished, hand engraved, gold lined; height, 3 inches. Price....................$1.00

No. 5R7143 Child's Cup, satin finished, hand engraved, gold lined; height, 2¾ inches. Price....................90c

No. 5R7146 Child's Cup, satin finished, hand engraved, gold lined; height, 2¼ inches. Price....................50c

No. 5R7148 Child's Cup, satin finish, gold lined, engraved; height, 3 inches; ornamented border and handle, something beautiful. Each................$2.25

No. 5R7151 Cup and Saucer, engraved, gold lined, satin finish. Each...............$2.75

No. 5R7154 Mustache Cup and Saucer, very fancy saucer, gold lined, engraved and ornamented border, satin finish. Each...............$3.50

No. 5R7155 Mustache Cup and Saucer, gold lined, beautifully hand engraved and satin finished. Each...............$4.50

Postage extra on plain band napkin rings, boxed, ready for shipment, 4 cents; fancy rings, toothpick holders and cups, about 8 cents; cups and saucers, about 12 cents. Silverware takes first class express and freight rates. See front of book for further instructions.

NAPKIN RINGS

FROM

15 CENTS TO $1.65.

No. 5R7160 Napkin Ring, satin finish, engraved, figure of man; height, 3 inches. Each............95c

No. 5R7163 Napkin Ring, figure of a dog, satin finish, hand engraved; height, 3¼ inches. Each.............$1.10

No. 5R7166 Napkin Ring, hand engraved, satin finish, gold lined. Each...............$1.65

No. 5R7169 Napkin Ring, satin finish, hand engraved. Each.....15c

No. 5R7172 Napkin Ring, plain, hand chased. Each...........30c

No. 5R7175 Napkin Ring, hand engraved, bare foot boy; gold lined, satin finish. Each, $1.40

No. 5R7176 Napkin Ring. Very fancy, hand engraved; height, 2¾ in. Each............75c

No. 5R7181 Child's Napkin Ring, plain, hand chased. Each.......20c

No. 5R7184 Napkin Ring, satin finish, engraved "Father." Each..50c

No. 5R7187 Napkin Ring, satin finish, engraved "Mother." Each..50c

No. 5R7190 Napkin Ring, satin finish, and engraved, extra scroll design. Each..........65c

No. 5R7192 Napkin Ring, satin finish, hand engraved, fancy border. Each..........55c

No. 5R7194 Napkin Ring, satin finish, hand engraved. Each..........45c

No. 5R7196 Napkin Ring, satin finish, hand engraved, fancy border. Each........75c

No. 5R7198 Fancy Napkin Ring, satin finished, engraved; height, 2¼ inches; fancy base. Each............... 75c

No. 5R7200 Fancy Napkin Ring; height, 2¼ inches; hand engraved, raised ornamented base. Each........85c

No. 5R7202 Fancy Napkin Ring; height, 3 inches; satin finish, engraved, carved man and dog. Each..........$1.00

No. 5R7204 Fancy Napkin Ring, satin finish, engraved, fancy base; height, 2 inches. Each..........$1.25

No. 5R7206 Fancy Napkin Ring, satin finish, hand engraved; height, 3 inches. Each.................80c

Page from 1902 Edition of The Sears, Roebuck Catalogue, showing quadruple plate mustache cups and saucers (notice original prices).

CUPS AND SAUCERS.

QUADRUPLE PLATE.

No. B5. Cup and Saucer.
Satin, Gold Lined....................................... $4 00
Satin, Bright Cut, Gold Lined............................. 4 50
No. B05. Same as above, Bright Cut, Gold Lined, with Mustache Guard.................................... 5 50

No. B6. Cup and Saucer.
Satin, Bright Cut, Gold Lined........................... $4 50
No. B06. Same as above, Bright Cut, Gold Lined, with Mustache Guard.................................... 5 50

No. S3506. Cup and Saucer, Bead Border.
Plain, Satin or Burnished................................ $4 40
Plain, Satin or Burnished, Gold Lined..................... 4 95

No. S3504. Cup and Saucer, Bead Border.
Plain, Satin or Burnished................................ $5 23
Plain, Satin or Burnished, Gold Lined..................... 6 05

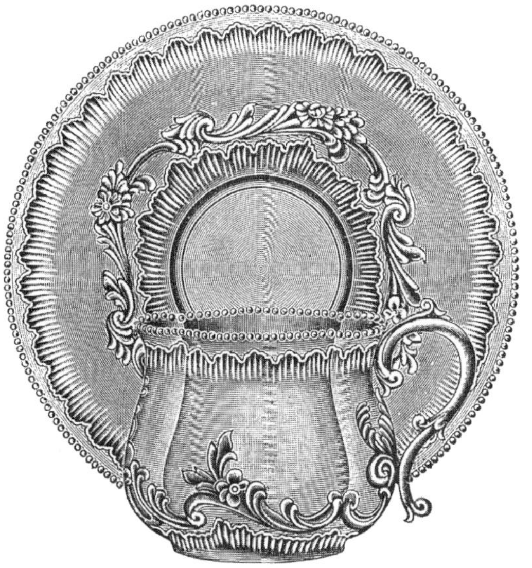

No. M3902. Cup and Saucer.
Gold Lined, Bright Embossed, Bead Border.............. $6 90

No. M1977. Cup and Saucer.
Gold Lined, Satin Engraved, Rococo Border.............. $6 60
Mustache Shield, extra.................................. 90

Page from 1896 Edition of The Marshall Field & Co. jewelry and fashions catalogue, showing quadruple plate cups and saucers.

Chapter Four

SETS AND GROUPINGS OF MUSTACHE CUPS

Chapter Four is devoted to sets and groupings of ceramic mustache cups, with or without saucers. The first and more readily found are sets of "His and Hers" cups, the "His" naturally sporting a mustache guard. Commemorative, wedding, and husband/wife sets fall into this category. Only one pictured set is inscribed "Husband" and "Wife." All other His and Hers sets are unlabeled. One wonders, tongue nestled in cheek, did the proper Victorians also have "significant others?" If so, the unlabeled sets were certainly discreet!

Matching pairs of left-handed cups and pairs of right-handed cups are included in this chapter. You'll also find an example of a pair of matching left- and right-handed mustache cups. However, this set is contemporary (1940+), not antique. A true Victorian set is extremely rare.

The photographs of luncheon sets, i.e., mustache cup and saucer and a matching sandwich or dessert plate, are given a value as a three-piece set. The groupings that follow, showing a mustache cup and saucer with assorted matching pieces, certainly enhance the value of the mustache cups and saucers. However, as this book is devoted to mustache cups, values given are for the cups and saucers only. Valuing the other pieces is best left to the experts in each field.

Included in this chapter are two groupings of mustache cups and saucers for size comparison. The first picture shows a normal size coffee cup, a demitasse, and a miniature. The next shows an oversize cup with a miniature. The miniatures in the photos are not at all the same size. One is a souvenir cup and the other could have been a salesmen's sample or part of a doll's tea set. Whatever the source, miniature mustache cups are very hard to find. It took this collector forty years to find one!

Demitasse MC/S Set: country unkn, c. 1870-1880, His and Hers, HP, deep pink inside cups, slight wear, applied MG, unmarked, $600-650.

MC/S Set: country unkn, c. 1891-1910, His and Hers, HP, brandy snifter shape, pedestals, much wear on gold, applied MG, mark unreadable, $400-700.

MC/S Set: country unkn, c. 1870-1880, His and Hers, HP, slight wear on gold, four-footed, applied MG, unmarked, $450-500.

MC/S Set: Austria, c. 1895-1917, modified His and Hers, HP, striking Alhambra geometric dsn, applied MG, Mark 97, $700-800.

MC Set: country unkn, c. 1902-1910, com, His and Hers (Queen Alexandra & King Edward VII), HP and decals, prized pink lustre, applied MG, unmarked, $400-450.

Kettle MC Set: country unkn, c. 1875-1885, rare Wedding Set, HP, grape leaves dsn, scalloped rims, cobalt on Hers only, four-footed, wear on gold, applied MG, unmarked, $400-800.

MC Set: Germany, c. 1887-1897, rare Husband and Wife, HP, raised dsn, applied MG, Mark 45, $700-750.

MC/S Set: country unkn, c. 1891-1925, matching left-handed MCs, one unmatched saucer, HP wedding band dsn, scalloped, applied MGs, unmarked, $400-500.

MC Set: country unkn, c. 1870-1879, modified matching right-handed MCs, HP wedding band dsn, rare raised and molded MGs, unmarked, $500-650.

MC/S Set: England, c. 1940+, matching left- and right-handed MCs, applied MGs, Mark 99, $250-300.

MC/S Set: Germany, c. 1892-1910, modified matching right-handed MCs, HP and transfer dsn, some wear, applied MGs, marked "OG, Germany," $375-425.

MC/S Set: Germany, c. 1891-1910, souv luncheon set, transfer dsn, applied MG, Mark 100, $300-350.

MC/S Set: Germany, c. 1887-1902, luncheon set, HP with gold beading, half-scissors handle, applied MG, Mark 25, $600-650.

MC/S Set: Germany, c. 1891-1900, luncheon set, transfer dsn, pedestal cup, serious chips, applied MG, Mark 33, $100-400.

MC/S Set: Germany, c. 1901-1910, fig luncheon set, HP and decal, rare twisted handle, rare cup shape, applied MG, Mark 101, $600-650.

MC/S Set: country unkn, c. 1870-1890, luncheon set, personalized with initials "WJ," HP and transfer dsn, slight wear on gold, applied MG, unmarked, $600-650.

MC/S Set: France, c. 1879-1889, luncheon set, HP and transfer, whimsical dsn, applied MG, Mark 120, $1,000-1,200.

MG: whimsical fly dsn, preceding MC.

MC/S Set: England, c. 1911, luncheon set, outstanding HP and transfer dsn, very deep saucer, applied MG, Mark 102, $950-1,100.

MG: matching HP cobalt and gold dsn, preceding MC.

MC/S Grouping: country unkn, c. 1870-1890, matched grouping, HP and transfer, pink and copper lustre, bamboo handle, applied MG, unmarked, $200-250 (MC/S only).

MC/S Grouping: England, c. 1908, matched grouping, swag dsn, Countess Pattern, applied MG, Mark 103, $400-450 (MC/S only).

MC/S Grouping: country unkn, c. 1875-1885, matched grouping, HP, unusual mold dsn, applied MG, unmarked, $200-250 (MC/S only).

MC/S Grouping: England, c. 1892-1910, outstanding HP and transfer dsn, much cobalt/gold, octagonal, unique handle, applied MG, Mark 104 (early Shelley), $500-550 (MC/S only).

MC/S Grouping: England, c. 1888, matched grouping (one MC/S—coffee; one MC/S—tea), HP and transfer ivy pattern, applied MGs, Mark 105, $850-1,000 (MCs/Ss only).

MC/S Grouping: England, c. 1873-1890, matched grouping, transfer dsn, deep saucer, applied MG, Mark 108, $350-375 (MC/S only).

MG: raised, transfer dsn, preceding MC.

MC/S Grouping: England, c. 1880, matched grouping (one MC/S; one regular demitasse C/S), HP and transfers, Beatrice Pattern, applied MG, Mark 106, $400-450 (MC/S only).

MC/S Grouping: country unkn, c. 1880-1890, similarities grouping (all pres; *left* and *right* cups are MCs; *center* cup a Hers w/no saucer), HP, blown-out molds, applied MGs, unmarked, $900-1,000 (set).

MC/S Grouping: country unkn, c. 1880-1890, similarities grouping (shapes, colors), all HP, applied MGs, unmarked, $800-850(set).

MC/S Grouping: country unkn, c. 1870-1880, similarities grouping (all same mold; dsn; two His and one Hers), applied gold dsn, applied MGs, unmarked, $850-950 (set).

MC/S Grouping: countries unkn (*left*—similar to gaudy Dutch), c. 1870-1880, similarities grouping (all octagonal; same mold; same twisted rope handle), HP, different dsns, applied MGs, unmarked, $900-1,100 (set).

MC/S Grouping: for size comparison only; from *left to right*—average MC/S, demitasse MC/S, miniature MC/S. Each one is pictured separately in Chapter One.

MC/S Grouping: for size comparison only; from *left to right*—farmers', MC/S, miniature MC/S. Each one is pictured separately in Chapter One.

MC/S Grouping: a lighted mirrored cabinet, with glass doors that lock, is one way to store and display a mustache cup collection. Note the salt dishes tucked in here and there to fill small spaces.

Chapter Six

MARKS/BACKSTAMPS

Chapter Six presents many of the marks/backstamps found on the ceramic mustache cups and/or saucers pictured in this book. Sometimes marks appear on cups or saucers only. Sometimes both pieces have identical markings. Occasionally, one piece of the set will have double markings. One mark might be that of the manufacturer and the other of the distributor or the artist. But many cups and saucers bear no markings at all.

When marks found on different cups are almost identical or have very close similarities, the caption directs you to see the comparable markings. Frequently the differences are as simple as a change in the color of the marks. Some marks found on the cups could not be photographed for various reasons such as clarity or condition.

The marks are numbered to coordinate with the general order of presentation of the cups from which they were photographed. Identical marks that are found on a number of cups are pictured only once. Captions that accompany each photographed cup direct you to the appropriate mark, if any.

Some marks may be difficult to read; others may be unfamiliar to you. Therefore, each caption repeats the wording of the actual mark in all capital letters. It also includes a brief description, when known. Marks found on mustache cups represent many different manufacturers in many different countries. They also cover a time span of much more than a hundred years. Therefore, dating the cups precisely is very difficult. Where possible, we tried to keep to a ten-year span.

Mustache cups made in the USA are very hard to identify as they were rarely marked. If you find one, treasure it! Marks etched or incised on silverplated mustache cups could not be photographed. Such marks are addressed in Chapter Three along with the cups.

Now that you know "all that there is to know" about marks on mustache cups, go on a mustache cup safari. But don't forget to arm yourself with the proper equipment—eyeglasses, magnifying glasses, a loop, a dictionary of marks that covers 1830-1999, and this guide, of course. Don't leave home without it!

Mark 1: France, CFH (Charles Field Haviland) /GDM (Gerard Dufraisseix, & Morel), underglaze, green; CH. FIELD HAVILAND, LIMOGES, overglaze, red, c. 1891-1900.

Mark 2: Germany, ROSENTHAL, crown and HAND PAINTED, c.1907-1920.

Mark 3: country unkn, crossed arrows and BLUE ONION in script, c. 1900+.

Mark 4: France, ELITE/L, FRANCE (Limoges), underglaze, green, sgn & dated, c. 1900-1903.

Mark 5: Germany, PK SILESIA and eagle, underglaze, dark green, c. 1880-1900.

Mark 6: Germany, KPM (Kranichfeld Porcelain Manufactory), GERMANY, underglaze, green, c.1903-1913.

Mark 7: country unkn, ROSE CROWN, overglaze, gold, c. 1900+.

Mark 8: USA, ROYAL CROWN®, underglaze, blue, c. 1949+.

Mark 9: Germany, K (Kahla Porcelain Factory), KAHLA, GERMANY, underglaze, red-brown, c. 1890.

Mark 10: Germany, J&C (Jaeger & Co.), MALMAISON, underglaze, blue-green, GERMANY, overglaze, red, c. 1902.

Mark 11: Japan, HAND PAINTED, NIPPON w/rising sun, overglaze, blue-green, c. 1890-1921.

Mark l2: country unkn, TM (intertwined) 1885, underglaze, black, c. 1885-1890.

Mark 13: Germany, rare RS (Reinhold Schlegelmilch) wing mark, GERMANY, overglaze, red-brown, c. pre World War I.

Mark 14: France, LIMOGES, FRANCE, with bird, underglaze, green; GD&C (G. Demartine & Co.), LIMOGES, FRANCE, overglaze, green, c. 1891-1904.

Mark 15: England, ROYAL WORCESTER, ENGLAND, overglaze, pink, c. 1889.

Mark 16: France, H&Co. (Haviland & Company) /L (Limoges), underglaze, green; HAVILAND & Co. LIMOGES, overglaze, blue, c. 1876-1889.

Mark 17: France, P&B, LIMOGES, FRANCE, overglaze, red; LIMOGES, arrow, FRANCE (on cup), underglaze, green, c. 1896-1905.

Mark 18: France, (on saucer), see Mark 17.

Mark 19: France, T&V (Tressman & Vogt), FRANCE, underglaze, green; sgn and dated (on cup), c. 1891-1917.

Mark 20: France, (on saucer), see Mark 19.

Mark 21: England or USA, TRADEMARK (on applied sticker), overglaze, purple, c. 1863+ (England), 1876+ (USA).

Mark 22: Germany, R (pierced by arrow), MADE IN GERMANY, overglaze, red, c. 1887+.

Mark 23: England, ROYAL STAFFORDSHIRE CERAMICS, ENGLAND (on cup), underglaze, brown, c. 1930+.

Mark 24: England, (on saucer), see Mark 23.

Mark 25: Germany, T (Tettau), GERMANY, Sontag & Sons (Royal Bayreuth), underglaze, green, c. 1887-1902.

Mark 26: Germany, R.C., IRIS, BAVARIA, Philip Rosenthal & Co., overglaze, green, c. 1901-1910.

Mark 27: Germany, ES (Erdmann Schlegelmilch), DEPON (registered) 3352, overglaze, brown, c. 1891-1900.

Mark 28: England, diamond shape registry mark and E.I.D.S., overglaze, blue, c. 1876.

Mark 29: France, ELITE WORKS (Bawo & Dotter), LIMOGES, FRANCE, overglaze, red; ELITE/L, FRANCE, underglaze, green, c. 1900-1914.

Mark 30: France, J. McD. & SONS, LIMOGES, overglaze, red; LIMOGES (in star), FRANCE, underglaze, green, c. 1891-1914.

Mark 31: England, PARAGON FINE BONE CHINA (now Royal Doulton Tableware), MADE IN ENGLAND, underglaze, black, c. 1920+.

Mark 32: England, MINTON, ENGLAND, underglaze, red, c. 1891-1900.

Mark 33: Germany, MANUFACTURED IN GERMANY, overglaze, brown, c. 1891-1900.

Mark 34: France, ELITE, SM (Bawo & Dotter), LIMOGES, FRANCE, overglaze, red; MR (M. Redon), FRANCE, underglaze, green, c. 1896-1900.

Mark 35: Italy, 704 ITALY, overglaze, brown, c. unkn.

Mark 36: England, ROYAL WORCESTER, ENGLAND, underglaze, blue, c. 1892-1899.

Mark 37: Germany, BAVARIA, LA REINE, underglaze, red; HAND PAINTED, underglaze, green, c. 1880-1890.

Mark 38: France, THEODORE HAVILAND, LIMOGES, FRANCE, PATENT APPLIED FOR, underglaze, green; artist sgn, A.C., overglaze, gold, c. 1904-1920.

Mark 39: Germany, K, BAVARIA (Purchasing Company for using Royal Bayreuth for advertising), overglaze, aqua, c. 1887-1902.

Mark 40: France, LIMOGES (early Bawo & Dotter mark), underglaze, red, c. 1870-1885.

Mark 41: France, CFH/GDM (see Mark I), FRANCE, underglaze, green; hand-lettered date, c. 1893.

Mark 42: Germany, DEPON (registered) 3977, underglaze, brown, c. 1891-1900.

Mark 43: England, ROYAL WORCESTER, underglaze, blue, c. 1882.

Mark 44: Oriental, country and mark unkn, underglaze, blue, c. 1880-1890.

Mark 45: Germany, MADE IN GERMANY, underglaze, dark green, c. 1891-1897.

Mark 46: France J.P./L. (Jean Pouyat/ Limoges), PATd. 3rd JAN. '93, FRANCE, underglaze, green, sgn, gold, c. 1893-1903.

Mark 47: Japan, HAND PAINTED NIPPON, M (Morimura Bros., importer), underglaze, green, c. 1891-1921.

Mark 48: Germany, R. S. PRUSSIA (Reinhold Schlegelmilch), underglaze, red and green wreath mark, c. 1880-1910.

Mark 67: England, W & SONS (H.M. Williamson & Sons), Rd. 265542, underglaze, green, c. 1895-1896.

Mark 68: Germany, (see Mark 62), c. 1891-1910.

Mark 69: Germany, DRESDEN, underglaze, blue, c. 1883-1893.

Mark 70: Germany, (see Marks 62, 68), c. 1891-1910.

Mark 71: country and mark unkn, c. pre-1891.

Mark 72: Germany, MADE IN GERMANY, W. W. ALLEN, PETACOOK, N. H., underglaze, green, c. 1891-1910.

Mark 73: Germany, MADE IN GERMANY FOR ARTHUR HIRSCH, (see Mark 81), underglaze, blue, c. 1918-1925.

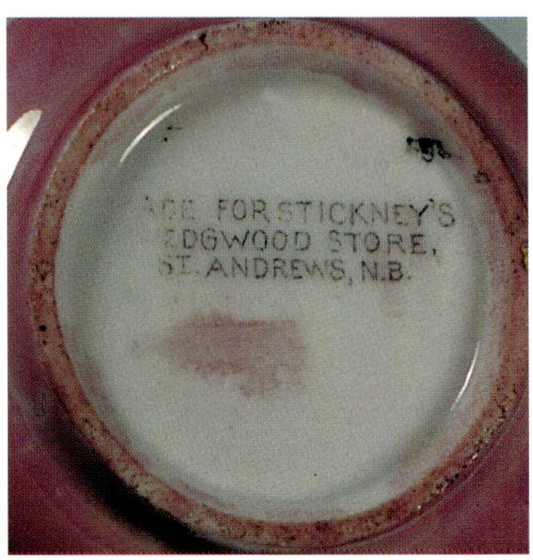

Mark 74: country unkn, MADE FOR STICKNEY'S WEDGWOOD STORE, ST. ANDREWS, N.B., overglaze, black, c. 1891-1910.

Mark 75: England, BROWNFIELD & SONS, TRADEMARK, ENGLAND, underglaze, red, c. 1871-1891.

Mark 76: Germany, MADE IN GERMANY, REDINGTON & Co., WATERVILLE, MAINE, underglaze, green, c. 1891-1910.

Mark 77: Germany, MADE IN GERMANY, STARR & BAILEY, GREENWICH, R.I., underglaze, green, c. 1891-1910.

Mark 78: Germany, MADE IN GERMANY, CHAS. A. ROSS, SKOWHEGAN, MAINE, underglaze, green, c. 1891-1910.

Mark 79: England, WEDGWOOD (Josiah Wedgwood), ENGLAND, underglaze, red, c. 1891-1904.

Mark 80: Germany, (see Marks 62, 68, 70), c. 1891-1910.

Mark 81: Germany, WEIMAR, GERMANY (see Mark 73), underglaze, blue, c. 1918-1920.

Mark 82: Germany, KAHLA, GERMANY (see Mark 9), c. 1890.

Mark 83: France, HAVILAND, FRANCE, overglaze, green; HAVILAND & Co., LIMOGES, underglaze, red, 1889-1905.

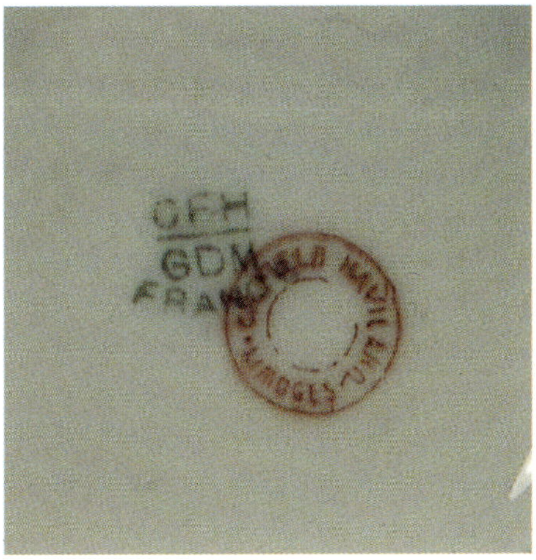

Mark 84: France, HAVILAND, LIMOGES (see Mark 1), c. 1881-1885.

Mark 85: Germany, EGLANTINE, GERMANY (Hermann Ohme Porcelain Manufactory), underglaze, green; sgn L.R., overglaze, red, c. 1882-1900.

Mark 86: Austria, VIENNA, overglaze, brown, c. 1885-1890.

Mark 87: England, ROYAL WORCESTER, JONES McDUFFEE & STRATTON, BOSTON, underglaze, green, c. 1887.

Mark 88: Japan, HAND PAINTED NIPPON, c. 1890-1921.

Mark 89: France, AK/D (A. Klingenberg/ Dwenger), underglaze, green; AK/CD (Klingenberg & Dwenger), LIMOGES, FRANCE, overglaze, red, c. 1890-1910.

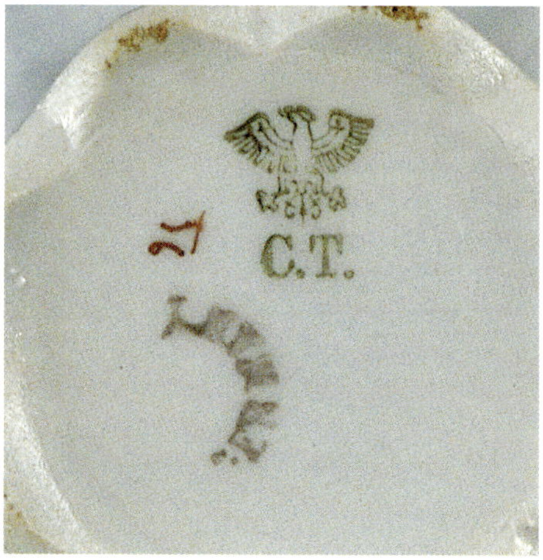

Mark 90: Germany, C.T. (C. Tielsch & Co.), underglaze, blue, c. 1875-1885.

Mark 91: Germany, T (Tettau, Royal Bayreuth), underglaze, green, c. 1887-1902.

Mark 92: Germany, R. S. PRUSSIA (see Mark 48), c. 1880-1910.

Mark 93: Japan, HAND PAINTED NIPPON (see Mark 60), c. 1891-1918.

Mark 94—fake: country unkn, fake R. S. Prussia mark, underglaze, red, c. unkn—reproduction.

Mark 95: Germany, PM, BAVARIA, overglaze, green, c. unkn.

Mark 96: country and mark unkn, overglaze mark superimposed on underglaze mark, blue, c. unkn.

Mark 97: Austria, mark unkn, underglaze, red, c. 1895-1917.

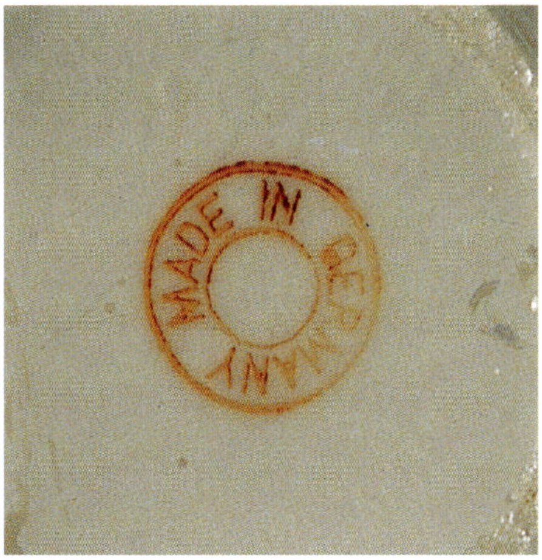

Mark 98: Germany, MADE IN GERMANY, overglaze, brown, c. 1887-1897.

Mark 99: England, HAMMERSLEY & Co., MADE IN ENGLAND, (now Royal Worcester Spode, Ltd.), underglaze, green, c. 1940+.

Mark 100: Germany, MADE IN GERMANY FOR J.C. LANDER, GARDINER, MAINE, underglaze, green, c. 1891-1910.

Mark 101: Germany, R.C. MONBIJOU (Philip Rosenthal & Co.), underglaze, green; HELIOS, GERMANY, overglaze, red, c. 1901-1910.

Mark 102: England, ROYAL CROWN DERBY, ENGLAND, underglaze, red, c. 1911.

Mark 103: England, ROYAL DOULTON, ENGLAND, Rd. No. 523784, COUNTESS (pattern), underglaze, green, c. 1908.

Mark 104: England, (Foley China Co., Longton, England, from the Wyler Collection), Pattern 3476, underglaze, red, c. 1892-1910.

Mark 105: England, Royal Worcester, Z (date letter), underglaze, green, c. 1888.

Mark 106: England, BEATRICE (pattern), TRADEMARK, WEDGWOOD & Co., underglaze, green, c. June 16, 1880.

Mark 107: Germany, MADE IN GERMANY (oversize mark), overglaze, black, c. 1892-1910.

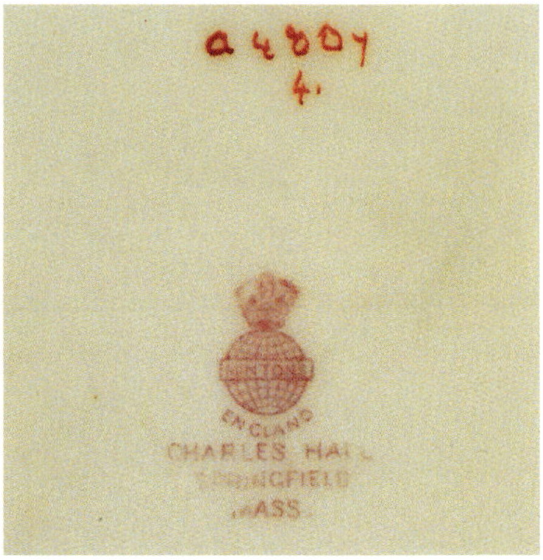

Mark 108: England, MINTON, ENGLAND (Royal Doulton Tableware), CHARLES HALL, SPRINGFIELD, MASS., overglaze, magenta, c. 1873-1890.

Mark 109: USA, AMERICANA, CURRIER & IVES, overglaze, green, c. 1930+.

Mark 110: England, LORD NELSON POTTERY, N, ENGLAND, overglaze, black, c. 1972.

Mark 111: England, WARRANTED 22-KARAT GOLD, underglaze, green, c. 1940+.

Mark 112: England, BONE CHINA, HAMMERSLEY & Co., MADE IN ENGLAND, (now Royal Worcester Spode, Ltd.), underglaze, green, c. 1940+.

Mark 113—fake: country unkn, BRANDENBURG, underglaze, blue, c. unkn—reproduction.

Mark 114—fake: country unkn, JP 1200, underglaze, blue, c. unkn—reproduction.

Mark 115: England, TRAFALGAWARE, STAFFORDSHIRE, ENGLAND (contemporary), overglaze, yellow, c. unkn—reproduction.

Mark 116: Germany, ROYAL BAYREUTH, PT, BAVARIA, overglaze, gold, c. 1902+.

Mark 117: Ireland, BELLEEK, CO. FERMANAGH, IRELAND, second black mark, printed, c. 1891-1926.

Mark 118: Germany, THREE CROWN CHINA, GERMANY, underglaze, black, c. 1891-1920.

Mark 119: Germany, BAVARIAN CHINA, GERMANY, underglaze, aqua, c. 1892-1912.

Mark 120: France, HAVILAND & Co. underscored, underglaze, green; R.E.S., factory artist's sgn, overglaze, red, c. 1876-1880.

Chapter Seven

Available Accessories

When mustaches were popular with dapper men of the Victorian Age, personal mustache cups were in great demand. And a whole new line of accessories became available through catalogues. Numerous brushes, combs, waxes, dyes, oils, and curlers were advertised as well as mustache spoons and portable mustache guards. The hirsute man had come into his own.

The earliest known mustache spoon was patented March 6, 1868, by Solon Ferrer of New York. Reed & Barton, silversmiths of Massachusetts, advertised a silverplated mustache spoon in their now famous 1885 catalogue. They reproduced this spoon in 1972 as a fun gift for men who wanted to keep pieces of soup vegetables out of their mustaches.

In the 1800s, mustache spoons (also known as etiquette spoons), were soupspoons designed to protect mustaches from particles of food collecting in and soiling their flowing adornments. They sported different kinds of mustache guards from fixed to removable for ease of cleaning. Mustache spoons were usually silverplated or sterling. A very few were designed for left-handed use. The only sterling silver left-handed mustache spoon these collectors have seen is pictured in this chapter!

One of the most ornate mustache spoons ever crafted was for *The California Midwinter International Exposition of 1894*. One recently sold at auction on eBay for several hundred dollars, a collector's dream come true. An artist's rendering of this spoon appears in this guide.

Victorians were noted travelers and collectors, especially fond of decorative knickknacks for their whatnots. Men who used their personal mustache cups and spoons for dining found it too tiring to tote them on trips of any length, or even for dining away from home. Voila! The portable mustache guard was invented. It came in a case to be easily carried in a gentleman's pocket. These portable guards were crafted in various shapes, designs, and materials. They were usually made of tin, pewter, silverplate, or sterling. Most were considered adaptable for right- or left-handed use. Some were advertised as being suitable for use on either cups or spoons. A number of mustache guards were shaped like a mustache; others had strainers to keep tea leaves from being ingested. These were not adaptable for use on spoons.

The earliest patent for a portable mustache guard was found in the U.S. Patent Office, dated 1885, and recorded under the category labeled "Cutlery." If a gentleman were to be found with one in his pocket today, might he be subject to arrest for "carrying a concealed weapon?"

This chapter pictures many of the accessories that were available for use by men with mustaches during the Victorian era. Captions will help you to identify the various items. One can't help but suspect that the Victorian men were as concerned with their hirsute facial adornments as were women with the crowning glory of hair on their heads. But that's a book for another day!

Victorian cup w/portable tin MG, Patented 10/29/01, in place for left-handed usage; identical portable MG is in front of cup; strainer portion of guards kept tea leaves from being imbibed.

Victorian cup w/portable MG
in place for right-handed use.

Victorian cup w/silverplated,
portable MG ready to be attached.

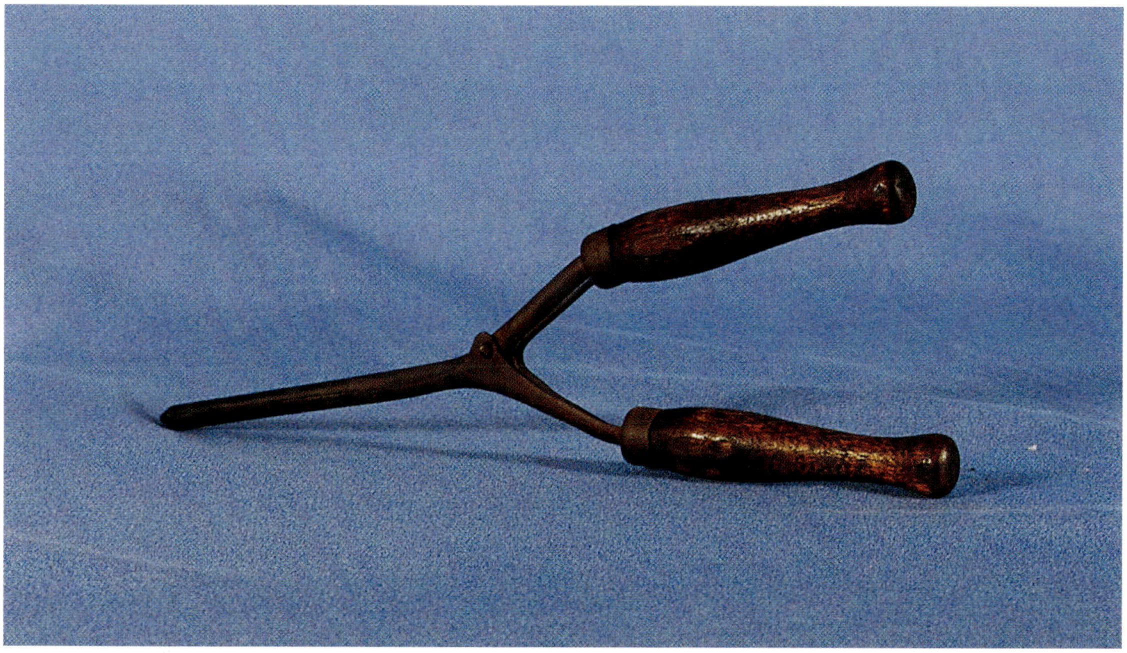

Mustache curling iron, wooden handles.

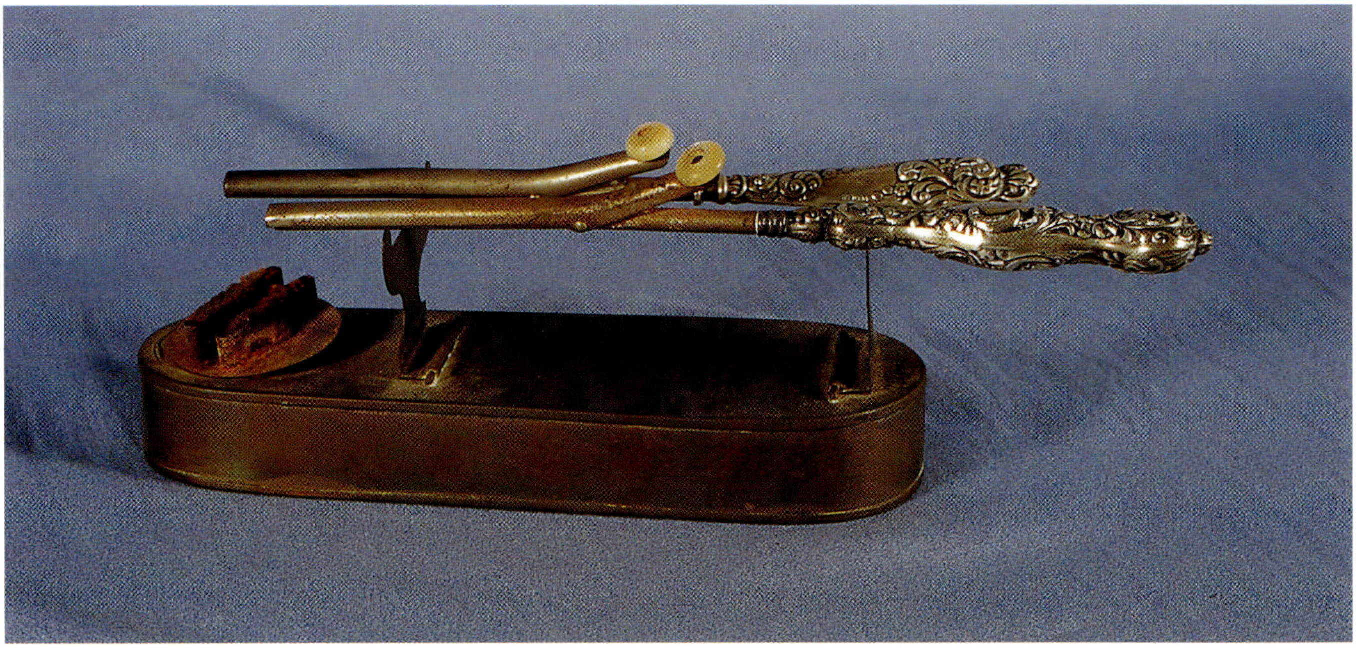

Portable spirit lamp, two sterling-handled curling irons.

Mustache brush, natural bristles set in bone, sterling silver handle.

Mustache brush, leather carrying case, embossed w/lion & unicorn coat of arms, on Victorian Limoges pin tray.

Different view of above brush on blue enameled tray.

Sterling silver mustache brush, monogram, "A.W.Y., Jr."

Tortoise shell mustache comb/case on Victorian Limoges pin tray.

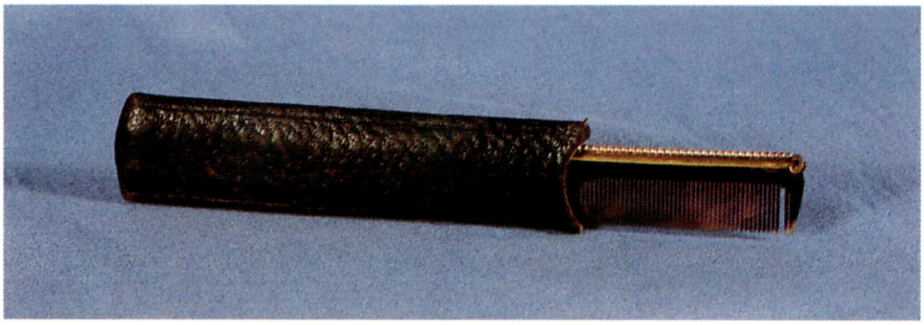

Tortoise shell mustache comb, w/case.

Tortoise shell pocket beard and mustache comb, silverplated case, engraved w/figures, marked, "Made in Denmark," on blue enameled tray.

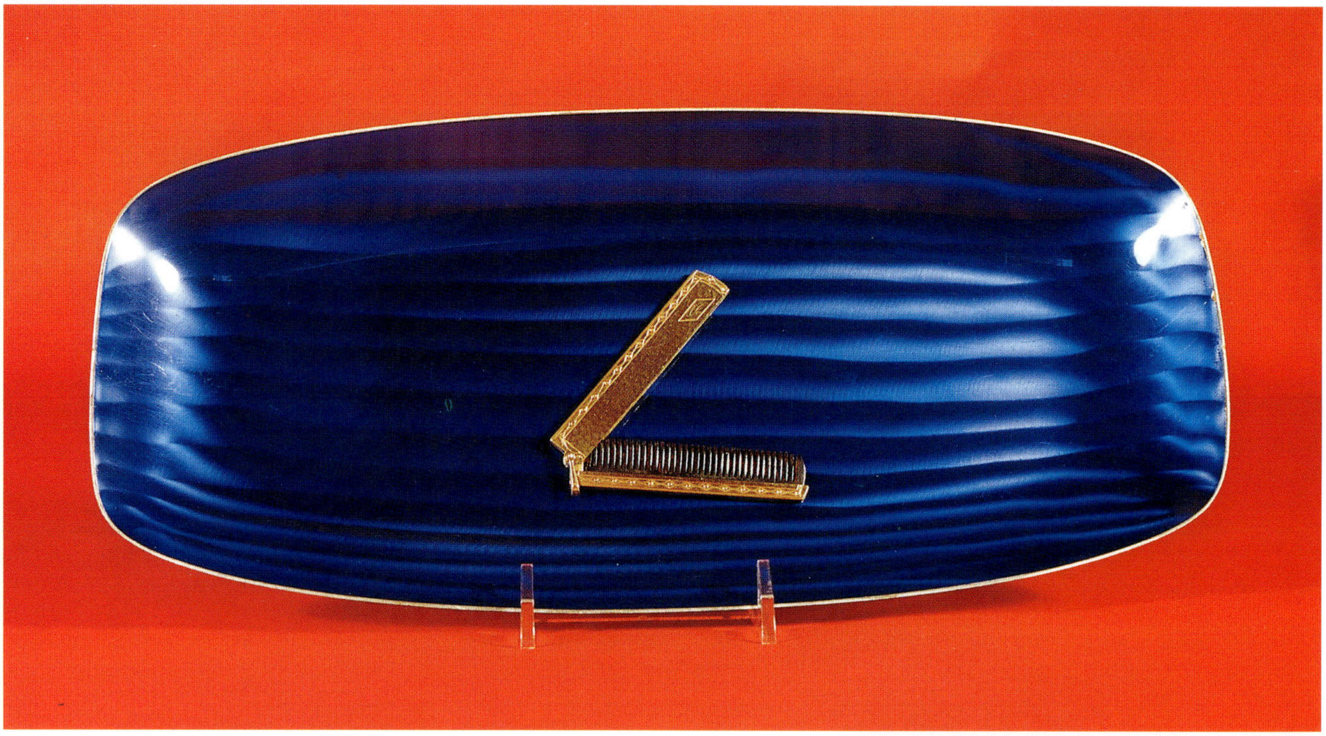

Folding celluloid mustache comb, gold-plated case, monogram, "D," marked, "Made in USA," on blue enameled tray.

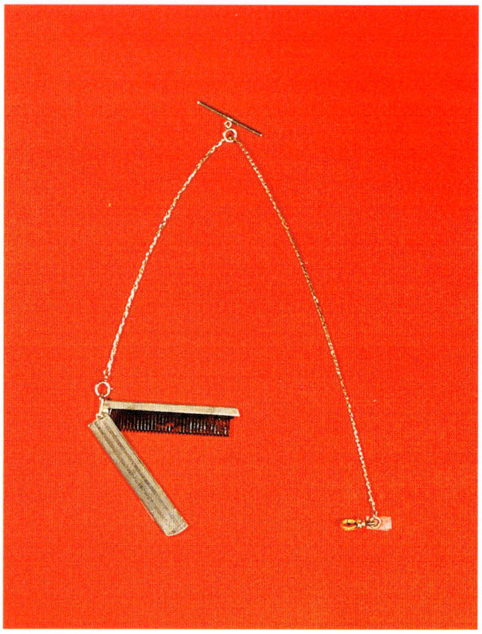

Folding tortoise shell mustache comb, gold-filled case, watch fob and chain.

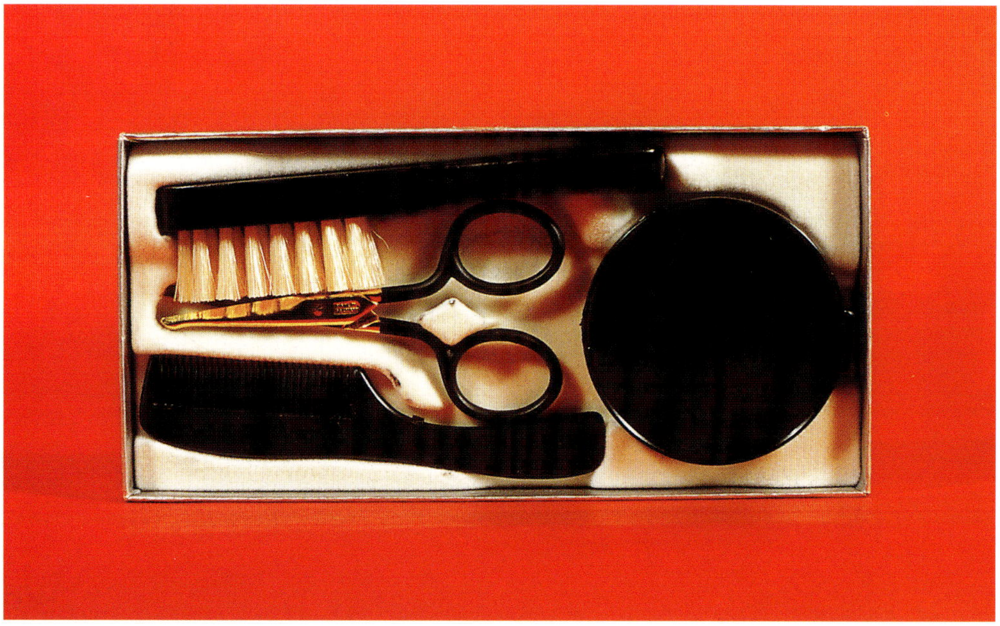

Reproduction mustache grooming set (brush, comb, mirror) w/original box, marked, "Made in W. Germany."

Reproduction silverplated mustache spoon, USA, c. 1972, fixed MG, Reed & Barton.

Silverplated mustache spoon, USA, c. 1893, engraved, "YEA SOUP—E.S. Grant, Xmas, '93," fixed MG, Reed & Barton.

Left:
Very rare, left-handed sterling silver mustache spoon, USA, c. 1895-1900, monogram, "W. E.," fixed MG, silversmith unkn, Patented 1895.

Below:
Two soup bowls and spoons, sterling silver regular soupspoon (*left*); quadruple plate mustache spoon, Reed & Barton (*right*).

Soup bowl and quadruple plate mustache spoon, USA, c. 1892-1897, hinged opening, silversmith unkn, Patented 1892.

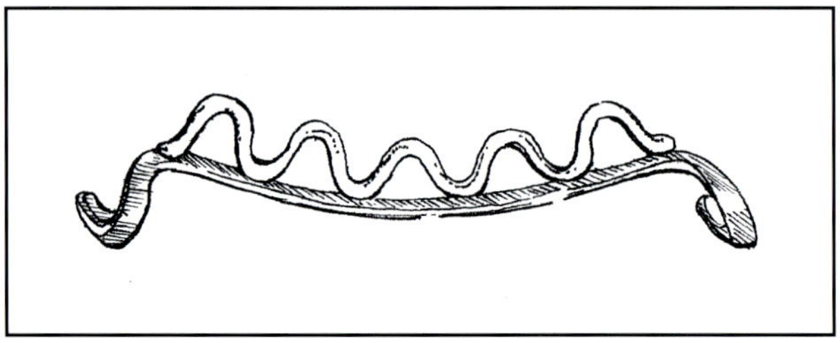

Artist's rendition, rare sterling silver portable MG, marked, "C.D. Peacock."

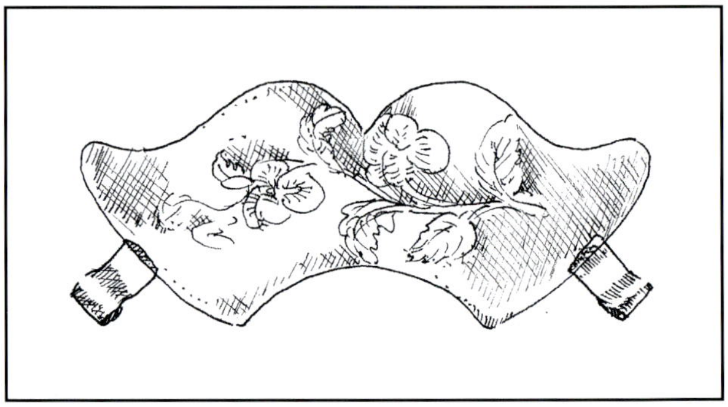

Artist's rendition, rare quadruple plate portable MG, engraved with pansies and leaves, marked, "Pat. Jan. 12,'97."

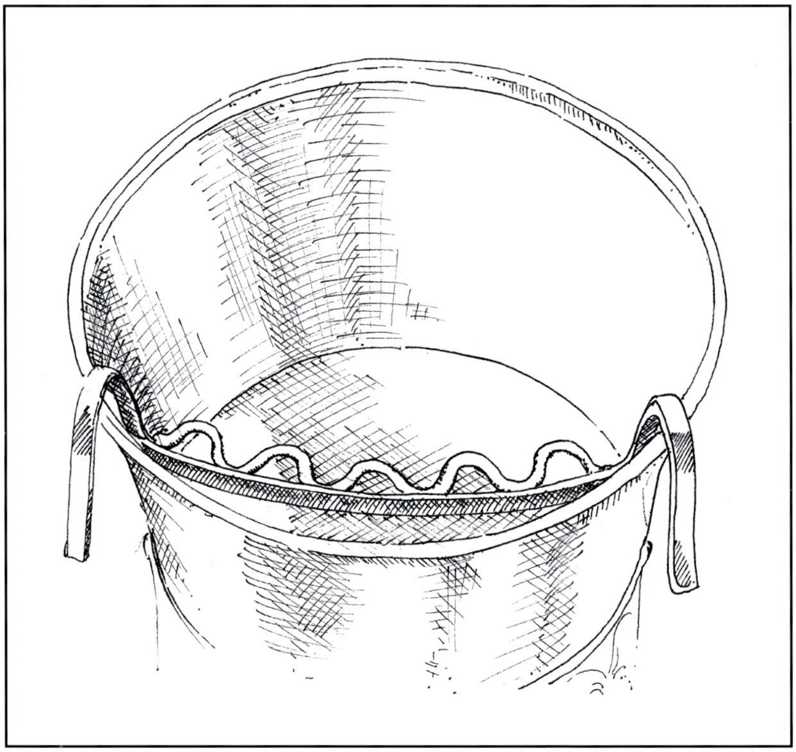

Artist's rendition, sterling silver portable MG attached to silver cup.

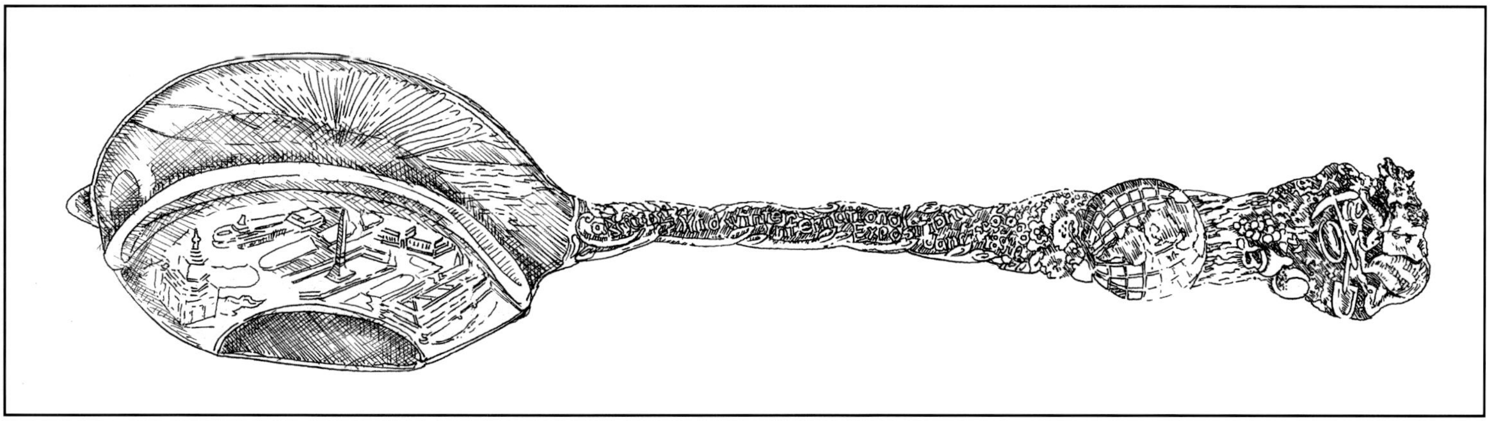

Artist's rendition, rare, very ornate mustache spoon, com, made for
The California Midwinter International Exposition of 1894.

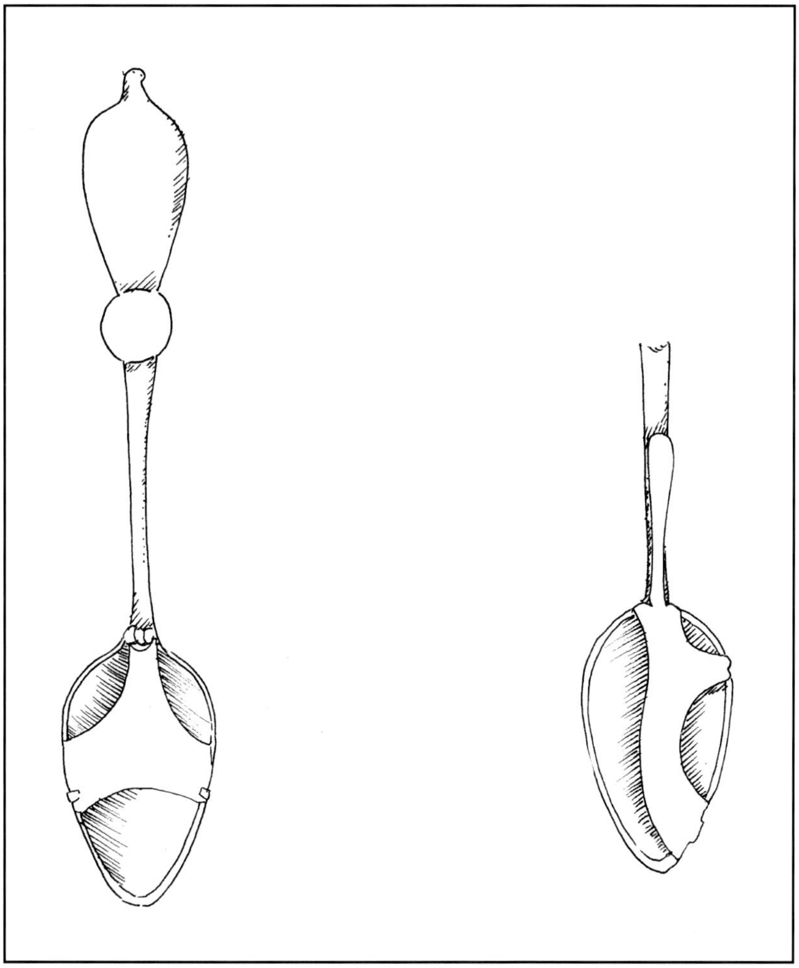

Artist's rendition, two mustache spoon designs, patented
Julius Berfels, Newark, New Jersey, May 6, 1884.

GLOSSARY

In this glossary you will find some words and phrases that are as comfortable as an old pair of shoes. Pass these by unless you have the urge to see how they fit in a new setting. Other terms will be new to you, especially in the context of mustache cups. Look them over. Say them. Listen to them. Then try them on for size! They will feel a bit stiff at first, but as you break them in, they too will soon be as comfortable as an old pair of shoes.

Add these terms to your various vocabularies. Trot them out frequently and use them in conjunction with the mustache cups you own, are thinking of purchasing, or are wishing to sell. Being knowledgeable in discussing mustache cups with other collectors or dealers will be beneficial.

accessories. Additional items that may be used with the item or items being described—gloves are accessories that may be worn with a hat.

applied. Something made separately and attached to another item. Most moustache guards and handles of mustache cups are applied.

ambiguous mark. A mark or backstamp that cannot be traced definitely to a particular manufacturer such as "crown" marks and "royal" marks.

Art Deco. A modernistic style of decoration that peaked around 1925 in Europe and America. Its geometric designs using circles, squares, rectangles, cones, and cylinders in bold colors were very popular.

artifacts. Simple objects (such as a tool or ornament) showing human workmanship and are products of civilization.

Art Nouveau. A style of decoration used during the "new art" period of 1885-1925. Artists tended to employ free-flowing designs and bold colors in place of realism.

backstamp. A mark that can be found under or overglaze on the bottom of a mustache cup and or saucer. The mark usually identifies the manufacturer and country of origin. The words, color, and design of a particular mark can also provide clues to the age of a piece. Many unmarked mustache cups had a paper label that wore off or was removed; some cups were never marked.

bisque. Identical to bisquit; also used by collectors and dealers when referring to a matte finish.

bone china. Softer than hard-paste porcelain and a knife will scratch its surface. It is much less fragile and less liable to chip; is creamy in tint and equally as translucent as hard or soft-paste porcelain.

bisquit. Clay that has been fired but is not glazed.

blank. Unfinished bisque, such as a mustache cup that is without decoration or glaze. Blank mustache cups were often made in one country and decorated in another.

blown out. Used by dealers and collectors for ceramic pieces that have a molded relief pattern embossed by the mold in which the cup was shaped. (See also molded relief.)

blue onion. The onion pattern was designed in the early 1700s at the Meissen factory. It was a mixture of earlier Oriental designs. Part of the design was a stylized peach that was mistaken for an onion. The onion is usually blue, but can be found in pink and red.

breakfast set. Usually consists of a teapot (coffeepot), creamer, sugar bowl, two cups and saucers, a large breakfast pastry dish, and two smaller individual dishes.

Capodimonte. Relief style, brightly colored and defined pieces of porcelain first made at a factory in Naples in the mid 1700s. It was identified under Capo-di-Monte until the late 1800s when the factory merged with Societa Ceramica Richard of Milan, which continues today to manufacture fine porcelain pieces marked with a crest and wreaths under a blue crown with R. Capodimonte.

coalport. Mainly bone china and feldspar porcelain. Rich enameling on tablewares, etc. and gilded Rococo ornaments.

cobalt. A deep blue oxide often used in ceramic decoration. It is able to withstand the glazing kiln heat. Very useful for underglaze and transfer-printed wares. Items decorated with cobalt are highly prized by dealers and collectors.

commemorative. Design or decoration that is chosen to remember or honor a particular event or person in history.

copper lustre. A type of pottery made in Staffordshire during the l800s. The copper lustre effect is obtained by applying low carat gold over deep red earthenware that darkens the finish to a coppery lustre.

crazing. A term for the fine web-like cracks that cover the surface of a piece of china. It is usually caused by the expansion of body and glaze upon repeated heating and cooling. Many pieces of old earthenware show signs of crazing; some pieces are purposefully crazed to give an appearance of age.

cross-collectible. Any item that meets more than one area of interest is a cross-collectible. A mustache cup is a good example. A cup and saucer in fine condition is of value to a mustache cup collector. If it is old Limoges it is of interest to a Limoges collector. If left-handed, it is prized by a collector of left-hand items, and so on.

decal. See decalcomania.

decalcomania. A process for transferring pictures from prepared paper onto furniture, porcelain, glass, etc., using a photographic process. Popular in the mid 1800s, it has been modernized and shortened to the term decal.

dessert set. This usually consists of a teapot, coffeepot, or chocolate pot with a cream pitcher and a sugar bowl where warranted, cups and saucers, a large cake plate, and matching individual smaller dessert plates. When men were being served, quite often a mustache cup and saucer were included.

Dresden. The term used for the fine porcelains that were produced in Meissen and Dresden, Germany, from the early 1700s well into the 1800s.

earthenware. The most common and the least expensive type of china that is still made today. It evolved from the old salt-glaze stoneware that broke easily and wore down the silver cutlery used with it. Earthenware is a lighter weight, less dense, and less crude product that is near white in color.

etiquette spoon. See mustache spoon.

faience. Originally the French name for tin-enameled ware, probably from Faenza, an important Italian Majolica center. The ware was important throughout France in the 1800s until ousted by porcelain.

fairings. Items usually won or bought at fairs as a memento or souvenir of the event.

firing. Baking or cooking of clay ware.

Flow Blue. A ware produced by many Staffordshire potters. The name refers to the blurred or flowing effect of the cobalt decoration caused by introducing a chemical vapor into the kiln. Flow Blue was most popular from about 1825 to 1900.

figural cups. Depict several people in a particular setting mainly through use of transfers or decals for the decoration. Some were hand painted and some were a combination of decals and hand painting.

footed. During the Victorian era, cups were often footed. The feet, usually four in number, ranged from simple to ornate in style and decoration. Three-footed cups are rare and considered to be a valuable asset to a collection.

Geisha Girl porcelain. Wares feature colorful kimono-clad Japanese ladies in scenes of everyday Japanese life surrounded by flora, fauna, and mountain ranges. The forms in which the wares were produced reflected the late nineteenth and early twentieth centuries. Most pieces were hand painted over stenciled outlines. Beware of Geisha ware decorated with decals. Most of them are Czechoslovakian reproductions.

gilding. Gold trim often used profusely on mustache cups. It was usually applied after the final glazing to avoid possible discoloration.

glaze. A finish usually composed of silica, alumina, and flux that is applied to porcelain and some other pieces of china. It seals the pores and renders the china impervious to liquids.

gold overlay. Gold decoration that is fired separately after other decoration is completed—usually the matte gold finish on porcelain.

handles. Mustache cup handles were either applied (added to the basic mold) or molded (part of the basic mold). Molded handles are the rarest, and highly prized in a collection. Mustache cup handles range from a basic form to very ornate. The styles include bamboo, half-scissors, a cherub or angel, open or closed butterfly, an open fan, rope, twisted rope, and wishbone.

hard paste porcelain. Is considered true porcelain—porcelain made from clay using kaolin. It is white or has a bluish tint and produces a hard, translucent body when fired.

His and Hers cups. A matching pair of cups and saucers with the gentleman's cup sporting the mustache guard that makes it a mustache cup. The Hers cup from the set is often mistaken for a gentleman's shaving mug, especially if separated from the mustache cup.

Imari. A generic term covering a wide family of wares made in a number of Japanese villages. Imari is the name of the port from which the wares were shipped to Europe. The Chinese also made Imari wares with a few differences from the Japanese wares. Imari-type wares were also copied by Meissen and by some English potters. The most common type of Imari features a colorful design with panels of birds, florals, or people surrounding a central basket of flowers.

incised mark. A backstamp marking that is scratched into the surface of the clay.

Irish Belleek. A thin translucent porcelain that is named for the village in Ireland where it originated around 1859. It has an ivory colored glaze with a pearl-like lustre. The shamrock pattern is the most popular. The age of a particular piece can be determined by the style and color of the mark or backstamp.

kettle shape. Resembling the footed shape of the old large black kettles that were used over open fires for boiling water, cooking, and washing clothes.

left-handed cup. To accommodate left-handed gentlemen, cups with handles to the left of the mustache guard were created. Because many left-hand cups have been reproduced due to their rarity, finding an authentic one is a challenge.

left-handed spoon. Left-handed mustache spoons were used to keep the mustache from being soiled while dining on soup. These spoons appear to have been made only in the U.S. Some of the mustache guards were affixed to the spoon; some had hinges to allow ease of cleaning, and portable guards could be affixed to regular soupspoons.

Limoges. A city in France where many different manufacturers produce exquisite, often hand painted porcelain items. The companies include Haviland (Theodore, David, Robert, etc.), Tressman & Vogt (T & V), Bawo and Dotter, and J. Pouyat. The porcelain produced by these companies is commonly referred to as Limoges.

lip guard. See *mustache guard.*

lustre. A metallic type of coloring decoration that affords an iridescent effect. Lustre finishes were highly coveted during the Victorian era. Pink or magenta lustre was most popular.

Majolica. A heavy earthenware that is design-molded and decorated with bright colors. Victorian Majolica has a lead glaze. Almost every noted potter in the U.S. and abroad produced majolica pieces, but only a few marked their wares.

mark. Found under or overglaze on the bottom of a mustache cup and/or saucer. Usually identifies the manufacturer and country of origin. Can also be used in determining approximate age of an item. Many unmarked items once had a paper label that wore off or was removed; a good many mustache cups were never marked. (See also *backstamp.*)

matte. A dull glaze finish that does not reflect light.

McKinley Tariff Act of 1890. Went into effect on the first day in March, 1891, whereby every imported item had to be marked in English words with the name of the country of origin.

Meissen. The Royal Saxon Porcelain Works was founded in 1710 at Meissen, Saxony. In order to protect their fine porcelain from imitations, Meissen adopted the crossed swords mark.

miniatures. Miniature mustache cups and saucers are very rare. Some were probably salesmen's samples, some were souvenirs, and possibly some were part of children's tea sets.

molded relief. A pattern embossed on a cup by the mold in which the cup is shaped. Collectors and dealers often refer to this as "blown out."

mustache brush. A small brush used to groom a bushy or handlebar mustache.

mustache comb. A small comb often made of bone or tortoise shell used to keep a man's mustache neat. Gentlemen of the Victorian period often carried them in small leather or silver cases or as a watch fob.

mustache cup. A Victorian tea, coffee, or demitasse cup made around 1830-1930 with a mustache guard to protect a gentleman's mustache from staining or soiling. Mustache guards were part of the cups, either molded or applied. The man's mustache rested on the guard while he sipped his hot beverage from one semi-circular opening in the guard.

mustache curling iron. Used to curl the ends of long drooping mustaches cultivated by many Victorian gentlemen. After curling, wax was applied to keep the mustaches curled.

mustache guard. A fixed internal ledge with one small semi-circular opening that is attached to one side of a mustache cup, or a raised molded ledge with the opening that is part of the rim of a cup. The mustache guard was designed to protect a man's mustache from soiling. (See also *portable mustache guard.*)

mustache mug. See *mustache cup.*

mustache spoon. Usually a soupspoon made circa 1830-1930 that had an attached mustache guard to protect a gentleman's mustache from soiling when ingesting soup. (See also *portable mustache guard.*)

Napoleons and saucers. Original nickname for mustache cups and saucers. Following the Franco-Prussian War, many men sported a Napoleon, or small beards and mustaches.

Nippon. A name the Japanese people gave their country, not a manufacturer's name. However, fine examples of porcelain marked "Nippon" are referred to as Nippon. One must be very wary of Nippon marks or backstamps. Reproductions of these marks are rampant.

Noritake. Noritake pieces that most collectors refer to are those manufactured by the Noritake Co., during 1921-1941. Many are identical to Nippon marked pieces, but the word Japan is found in the mark or backstamp.

overglaze. A design, mark, decal, or backstamp that is applied to an item that has a fired glazed surface. The article can be re-fired to make the application permanent.

pewter. An alloy composed mainly of tin. Brightly polished, it is a less expensive tableware alternative to silver. During the eighteenth century, it was largely replaced by earthenware.

porcelain. The finest form of pottery. It is translucent and consists of three types—hard paste, soft paste, and bone china. It is not porous and thus does not craze like earthenware.

portable mustache guard. Made of metal (silver, silverplate, tin) and could be attached to regular cups or soupspoons. A portable mustache guard was carried by a mustachioed man for use away from home.

portrait cups. Mustache cups decorated with a portrait, usually of a Victorian lady. The majority of portraits are decals; although a very few were hand painted.

pottery. Includes all forms of wares made from clay, but acceptable as a term for earthenware and stoneware as distinct from translucent porcelain.

presentation cups. Were personalized cups from the giver through a name, initials, phrase, sentence, or even a poem. These could be in relief or handwritten on the outside of the cup. A few were on the mustache guards.

quadruple plate. Most silver mustache cups and saucers are silverplated. Research does not register any that were sterling silver. Quadruple plate refers to the highest ware constructed of silver, in contrast to sterling silver.

R.S. Germany. Reinhold Schlegelmilch began manufacturing porcelain in Suhl, in the German province of Thuringia, in 1869. In 1894, he opened another factory in Tillowitz, Upper Silesia. The wares produced here were usually marked "R.S. Germany."

R.S. Prussia. Porcelain marked "R.S. Prussia" was manufactured by Reinhold Schlegelmilch from the late 1870s to the early 1900s, in the Germanic area known as Prussia, until the end of World War I. Many reproductions have been and are still being made. Know your marks!

Royal Bayreuth. The name of a factory that was founded in Tettau, Bavaria, in 1794. The marks representing Royal Bayreuth have changed over the years. From about 1870 through 1919, a stylized crest and the words Bavaria and Royal Bayreuth have appeared in slightly different forms.

Royal Crown Derby. The Royal Crown Derby Company began manufacturing porcelain in 1848. After a number of name and ownership changes, the company merged with The Derby Crown Porcelain Co., Ltd. In 1890, the new company was appointed as a manufacturer for the Queen and began using the name Royal Crown Derby.

Royal Doulton. The name used on Doulton and Company pottery made from 1902 to the present. Doulton and Company of England was founded in 1853.

Royal Worcester. A name used by collectors. Worcester porcelains were made in Worcester, England, beginning about 1751. After going through different periods and name changes, the company became the Worcester Royal Porcelain Company, Ltd., in 1862. Collectors call the porcelain made after 1862 Royal Porcelain.

semi-porcelain. Stoneware. It is hard, dense, thin but not translucent, and needs a glaze. It has no relationship whatsoever to true porcelain.

shaving mugs. Very popular with most men from the mid 1800s through the early 1900s. There were many types of these mugs, including occupational (depicting men's jobs), scuttle mugs, silverplated mugs, glass-lined mugs, and others. Many featured initials or names and were kept at men's favorite barbershops. These mugs were for shaving only and were not in any way associated with mustache cups.

signed. Signed mustache cups and/or saucers are highly prized by collectors. Artist's signatures are usually hand-lettered or written and appear somewhere on the cup or saucer, often on the base. Presentation cups are frequently "signed" in a hand-lettered message on the base of the pieces. Some auctioneers and antique dealers refer to a piece as "signed" if it has a legible mark or backstamp.

soft paste porcelain. Looks like white enamel, is "soapy" to the touch, creamy in tint, and is more translucent than hard paste.

souvenir. Decoration on a cup and/or saucer that serves as a reminder of a place visited.

Staffordshire. A type of pottery made in England's Staffordshire district in the early 1700s. Several potteries remain and are still producing this ware.

stoneware. Vitreous like porcelain, but is always opaque due to the impurities present because the basic clay is unselected. Although dense, stoneware is porous if liquids are kept in it for a time. Therefore, it is usually glazed inside and out.

Sunderland lustre. The name given to a special kind of purple-pink lustre made in England in the 1800s.

The lustre is metallic and appears to have bubbles in it. It is often associated with sailor gifts during the early to mid 1800s. These wares also had black transfer printing. Many bore verses or personal inscriptions.

tea-and-toast. A term used for a cup and saucer set in which the saucer is large enough to hold a slice of toast as well as the teacup. A very rare square-shaped tea-and-toast is pictured in Chapter Four of this book.

transfers. A process of transferring a paper print onto an object. The paper was removed from the ware, leaving the pattern to be fixed by kiln firing. Originally black, two or more colors could be transfer-printed underglaze from 1830 on. Decalcomania transfers came into general use about 1880, but they were applied overglaze and were not reliably permanent. They rubbed off over time.

translucent. Not transparent, but allows rays of light to pass through an object.

underglaze. High temperature colors were used for ceramic decorations and marks or backstamps that could endure the heat of the glazing kiln. This was most important for tablewares in order to protect the pattern or mark from wear. Hard paste porcelains required even greater heat. The potters could use only cobalt blue and rare copper red to withstand the heat. All other colors had to be applied overglaze, fixed by a lesser kiln heat.

Victorian. A period named in honor of the long reigning British Queen, Victoria. The period roughly spans the years from about 1830 to about 1901. Although the Victorian era can be referred to as early, middle, and late Victorian, there are no sharp definitions.

Victoriana. Any item or style associated with the Victorian years.

Wedding Set. A gift to a bride and groom on their wedding day that comprised two cups and saucers—the bridegroom's being a mustache cup with saucer. These were usually highly decorated and often saved as a memento of the wedding day.

SELECTED BIBLIOGRAPHY

Preparations for writing this book about mustache cups involved more than the usual amount of research. Why? To date, according to all research, only one other book devoted to this Victorian collectible was ever written. And this book is out of print. Fortunately, I had acquired a copy many years ago. Unfortunately, it contains no price guide. So my fingers had to "do the walking" through the pages of many different sources and guidebooks to add their pertinent value figures to my pricing hopper.

Another contributing factor to lengthy research was the scarcity of information concerning the place and date of birth of the first mustache cup. According to one knowledgeable source, it was conceived, designed, and manufactured by one Harvey Adams in 1830, at Longton, Stoke-on-Trent, England. (See the History section to learn more about this porcelain invention.)

Spelling was also an impediment to the research process. History and my computer had a problem with mustache/moustache. At times, the computer would recognize mustache and serve me a smorgasbord of material. At other times, moustache was the menu of the day with fewer pertinent offerings.

One final problem was a case of mistaken identity. This cropped up more frequently than I would have guessed. A proper Victorian gentleman would have snickered up his sleeve to see his soapy shaving mug labeled a mustache cup and vice versa. Hopefully, this book will help to clear up this comic confusion.

Bockol, Leslie. *Victorian Majolica.* Atglen, Pennsylvania: Schiffer Publishing Ltd., 1998.

Boger, Louise Ade. *House & Garden's Antiques: Questions and Answers.* New York, New York: Simon and Schuster, 1973.

———. *The Dictionary of World Pottery and Porcelain.* New York, New York: Charles Scribner's Sons, 1971.

Collecting New Jersey Antiques. Union City, New Jersey: Wm. H. Wise & Co., Inc., 1989.

D'Imperio, Dan. *The ABC's of Victorian Antiques.* New York, New York: Dodd, Mead and Co., 1974.

Gaston, Mary Frank. *Collector's Encyclopedia of R. S. Prussia, Fourth Series.* Paducah, Kentucky: Collector Books, 1997.

———. *The Collector's Encyclopedia of Limoges Porcelain.* Paducah, Kentucky: Collector Books, 1997.

Godden, Geoffrey. *An Illustrated Encyclopedia of British Pottery and Porcelain.* New York, New York: Crown Publishers, 1966.

Haggar, Reginald G. *The Concise Encyclopedia of Continental Pottery and Porcelain.* New York, New York: Hawthorne Books, Inc., 1960.

Hammond, Dorothy. *Confusing Collectibles.* Des Moines, Iowa: Homestead Book Company, 1969.

———. *Mustache Cups, History and Marks.* Des Moines, Iowa: Wallace-Homestead Book Company, 1972.

Howe, Bea. *Antiques from the Victorian Home.* New York, New York: Scribner, 1973.

Huxford, Sharon, & Bob, Eds. *Schroeder's Antiques Price Guide*, Seventeenth Edition. Paducah, Kentucky: Collector Books, Schroeder Publishing Co., Inc., 1999.

Jacobsen, Gertrude Tatnall. *Haviland China, Volume One.* Des Moines, Iowa: Wallace-Homestead, 1979.

Kamm, Minnie Watson. *Old China.* Grosse Point Farms, Michigan: First Edition, 1951.

Kovel, Ralph and Terry. *Know Your Antiques.* New York, New York: Crown Publishers, Inc., 1967.

———. *Kovels' Antiques & Collectibles Price List 1997.* New York, New York: 1997.

———. *Kovels' Antiques & Collectibles Price List 1998.* New York, New York: Three Rivers Press, 1998.

———. *Kovels' Dictionary of Marks—Pottery and Porcelain 1650 to 1850.* New York, New York: Crown Publishers, Inc., 1995.

———. *Kovels' Know Your Antiques.* New York, New York: Crown Publishers Inc., 1981.

———. *Kovels' New Dictionary of Marks, Pottery and Porcelain 1850 to the Present.* New York, New York: Crown Publishers, Inc., 1986.

McCaslin, Mary J. *Royal Bayreuth, A Collector's Guide.* Marrietta, Ohio: Antique Publications, 1994.

McClinton, Katherine (Morrison). *Collecting American Victorian Antiques.* New York, New York: 1966.

Mesiere, Ernest, Editor. *Porcelain Theodore Haviland.* Paris, France: Haviland Company, 1912.

Miller, Judith and Martin. *Millers' World Encyclopedia of Antiques.* New York, New York: Viking Penguin, 1989.

Miller, Robert W. *Bicentennial Wallace-Homestead Price Guide to Antiques and Pattern Glass.* Des Moines, Iowa: Wallace-Homestead Book Company, 1975.

Orbach, Barbara Milo. *Antiques at Home.* New York, New York: Clarkson N. Potter, Inc., 1989.

Ormsbee, Thomas H. *Care and Repair of Antiques*. New York, New York: Gramercy Publishing Company, 1969.
Penkala, Maria. *European Porcelain: A Handbook for the Collector.* Second Edition. Rutland, Vermont: Charles E. Tuttle, 1968.
Platt, Dorothy Pickard. *The Story of Pickard China*. Hanover, Pennsylvania: Everybody's Press, Inc. 1970.
Rainwater, Dorothy. "Mustache Spoons." *The Spinning Wheel's Complete Book of Antiques*. New York, New York: Grossett & Dunlap, 1972.
Rontgen, Robert E. *Marks on German, Bohemian, and Austrian Porcelain: 1710 to the Present*. Exton, Pennsylvania: Schiffer Publishing Co., 1981.
Schull, Thelma. *Victorian Antiques*. Rutland, Vermont: Charles E. Tuttle Co., 1963.
Silver. "Mustache Guards and Cups." Whittier, California: Silver Magazine, Inc. May-June, 1992.
Tait, Hugh. *Porcelain*. New York, New York: Marboro Books, 1962.
Travis, Nora. *Haviland China: The Age of Elegance,* Revised 2nd Edition. Atglen, Pennsylvania: Schiffer Publishing Ltd., 1998.
The Lyle Official Antiques Review, 1997. The New Berkley Publishing Group, 1996.
Terrele, George W., Jr. *Collecting R.S. Prussia: Identification and Values*. Florence, Alabama: Books Americana, 1982.
Van Patten, Joan F. *The Collector's Encyclopedia of Nippon Porcelain*. Paducah, Kentucky: Collector Books, 1979, values updated 1997.
———. *The Collector's Encyclopedia of Nippon Porcelain,* Fourth Series. Paducah, Kentucky: Collector Books, 1997.
———. *The Collector's Encyclopedia of Nippon Porcelain*, Third Series. Paducah, Kentucky. Collector Books, 1986, values updated 1996.
———. *The Collector's Encyclopedia of Noritake*. Paducah, Kentucky: Collector Books, 1997.
Warman, Edwin G. *Twelfth Antiques and Their Current Prices*. Uniontown, Pennsylvania: E. G. Warman Publishing, Inc., 1974.
Weiss, Gustav. *Book of Porcelain*. Translated by Janet Seligman. New York, New York: Praeger Publishers, Inc., 1971.

INDEX